ILTS 229 Teacher of Students Who Are Deaf or Hard of Hearing

Iris Q. McKinley

This page is intentionally left blank.

This page is intentionally left blank.

Table of Content

This page is intentionally left blank.

Chapter 1 – Questions

QUESTION 1

A 10-year-old student with a profound hearing loss has been experiencing behavioral challenges in the classroom. The teacher notices that the student often becomes frustrated and acts out when they cannot fully participate in class discussions. Which of the following strategies is most appropriate to address the educational implications of this student's disability?

A. Assign extra homework to keep the student engaged.
B. Implement a peer buddy system to facilitate communication.
C. Recommend auditory training exercises after school.
D. Suggest a change of schools to a specialized program.

Answer:

QUESTION 2

A high school student with a hearing impairment is interested in pursuing a career in the performing arts. They excel in acting and dancing but are concerned about how their disability might affect their career prospects. What advice should a special education teacher provide to address the implications of their disability on their career aspirations?

A. Discourage pursuing a career in the performing arts due to communication challenges.
B. Recommend focusing solely on non-performing roles within the industry.
C. Encourage the student to pursue their passion and explore accommodations.
D. Advise the student to switch to a career in a different field.

Answer:

QUESTION 3

A middle school student who is deaf has been prescribed medication for a medical condition. The medication has potential side effects, including dizziness and fatigue. How might these side effects impact the student's learning and functioning in the classroom?

A. The side effects will have no impact on the student's learning.
B. The student may struggle to stay awake and focused in class.
C. The student will experience improved concentration.
D. The side effects will enhance the student's ability to learn.

Answer:

QUESTION 4

A 12-year-old student who is hard of hearing is experiencing difficulties in reading comprehension. The teacher suspects a learning disability in addition to the hearing impairment. What should be the initial step taken to address the educational implications of this situation?

A. Request immediate placement in a special education class.
B. Conduct a comprehensive assessment to identify specific learning needs.
C. Ignore the reading difficulties as they are unrelated to hearing loss.
D. Advise the student to rely solely on lip-reading for better comprehension.

Answer:

QUESTION 5

A high school student with a profound hearing loss is considering taking a medication with potential side effects that could affect their academic performance. As a special education teacher, what should you do to address the implications of this medication on the student's learning and development?

A. Encourage the student to stop taking the medication to avoid side effects.
B. Consult with medical professionals to understand potential accommodations.
C. Suggest the student increase the medication dosage for better results.
D. Advise the student to discontinue their education due to medication concerns.

Answer:

QUESTION 6

A 14-year-old student who is deaf is struggling with emotional and behavioral challenges in the classroom. The student often feels isolated and frustrated due to communication barriers. What proactive approach should a special education teacher take to address the educational implications of the student's emotional/behavioral challenges?

A. Isolate the student to prevent disruptions in the classroom.
B. Provide the student with hearing aids to improve communication.
C. Foster a supportive and inclusive classroom environment.
D. Advise the student to switch to a specialized school for behavior disorders.

Answer:

QUESTION 7

You are a special education teacher working with a deaf high school student named Sarah. Sarah has a strong interest in science and aspires to become a biologist. She has excellent academic skills but struggles with communication due to her hearing impairment. Sarah's parents are concerned about her future career prospects in science. How should you address this situation to support Sarah's educational and career goals?

A. Advise Sarah to abandon her dreams of becoming a biologist due to communication challenges.
B. Recommend enrolling Sarah in a special education program exclusively for deaf students.
C. Collaborate with the school's speech-language therapist to provide communication support.
D. Discourage Sarah from pursuing a career in science and steer her toward a different field.

Answer:

QUESTION 8

You are a special education teacher working with a hard of hearing student named Alex in a mainstream elementary school. Alex's academic performance has been steadily declining, and you suspect that it may be related to his hearing difficulties. How can you best address the situation and ensure Alex receives appropriate support?

A. Suggest transferring Alex to a specialized school exclusively for hard of hearing students.
B. Request additional time for Alex during exams to accommodate his hearing impairment.
C. Ignore the issue as hearing difficulties are unlikely to affect academic performance.
D. Recommend having Alex repeat a grade to catch up with his peers.

Answer:

QUESTION 9

You are a special education teacher working with a group of deaf and hard of hearing students in a high school. One of your students, Daniel, has been showing signs of emotional distress and frustration due to communication barriers with his peers. He often feels isolated and misunderstood. How should you address Daniel's emotional and social well-being within the school environment?

    A.   Isolate Daniel from the group to prevent further emotional distress.
    B.   Organize regular group counseling sessions for all deaf and hard of hearing students.
    C.   Provide Daniel with a sign language interpreter for all social interactions.
    D.   Suggest Daniel switch to a mainstream school for better social integration.

Answer:

QUESTION 10

A preschool-age child has recently been diagnosed with congenital hearing loss. Their parents are concerned about the child's future communication development. Which intervention is most likely to have a positive impact on the child's language development?

    A.   Delay any interventions until the child reaches school age.
    B.   Start sign language instruction immediately.
    C.   Enroll the child in a mainstream school without specialized support.
    D.   Encourage lip-reading practice exclusively.

Answer:

QUESTION 11

You are working with a middle school student who has acquired hearing loss due to a recent illness. The student is experiencing difficulties in understanding spoken instructions in the classroom. Which approach should you consider to support their learning?

    A.   Provide written instructions only.
    B.   Encourage the student to rely solely on lip-reading.
    C.   Advocate for additional classroom accommodations.
    D.   Advise the student to change to a different school.

Answer:

QUESTION 12

A high school student with hearing loss has expressed an interest in participating in sports, specifically basketball. The student's parents are concerned about potential safety issues. How can you address these concerns while supporting the student's aspirations?

    A.   Discourage the student from participating in sports due to safety risks.
    B.   Recommend enrolling the student in a deaf sports program.
    C.   Provide information on safety measures and equipment.
    D.   Advise the student to focus solely on academic pursuits.

Answer:

QUESTION 13

You are working with a young child who has hearing loss and has recently received cochlear implants. The child is experiencing frustration and anxiety during therapy sessions. What is the most appropriate approach to address these emotional challenges?

    A. Discontinue therapy to reduce stress.
    B. Increase therapy intensity to speed up progress.
    C. Provide emotional support and encouragement.
    D. Advise the parents to rely solely on the cochlear implants.

Answer:

QUESTION 14

A high school student with congenital hearing loss is interested in pursuing a career in music. What specialized accommodations or considerations should be made to support their musical aspirations?

    A. Encourage the student to pursue a different career path.
    B. Provide information on music programs exclusively for deaf individuals.
    C. Explore accommodations such as vibrating platforms for musical vibrations.
    D. Advise the student to rely solely on visual cues for music performance.

Answer:

QUESTION 15

You are working with a deaf high school student who has additional sensory and motor differences. The student is struggling with communication and mobility. What should be the first step in addressing these challenges?

    A. Recommend enrolling the student in a specialized school for students with multiple disabilities.
    B. Explore assistive technology solutions to improve communication and mobility.
    C. Advise the student to rely solely on sign language for communication.
    D. Encourage the student to withdraw from social interactions to reduce challenges.

Answer:

QUESTION 16

You are a special education teacher working with a group of deaf and hard of hearing students in a mainstream school. One of your students, Mia, uses sign language as her primary mode of communication. During a group discussion, Mia struggles to participate effectively. What should you consider to support Mia's participation in inclusive classroom activities?

    A. Encourage Mia to rely solely on lip-reading for communication.
    B. Provide written transcripts of class discussions in advance.
    C. Suggest Mia switch to a school exclusively for deaf students.
    D. Advise Mia to use sign language exclusively, even in mainstream settings.

Answer:

QUESTION 17

You are working with a hard of hearing student, Max, who experiences auditory fatigue and struggles to maintain attention during long lectures. What would be an appropriate strategy to address Max's needs and improve his classroom experience?

    A. Extend the duration of lectures to ensure comprehensive coverage.
    B. Provide frequent breaks during lectures to reduce auditory fatigue.
    C. Advise Max to use hearing aids with maximum volume at all times.
    D. Recommend Max sit in the back of the classroom for a quieter environment.

Answer:

QUESTION 18

A deaf high school student, Ben, has expressed a strong interest in pursuing a career in computer programming. What educational considerations should be made to support Ben's aspirations in the field of computer science?

    A. Discourage Ben from pursuing computer science due to communication challenges.
    B. Provide opportunities for Ben to explore computer programming languages.
    C. Advise Ben to focus exclusively on written coding and avoid collaborative projects.
    D. Recommend a career change for Ben to a field with less reliance on communication.

Answer:

QUESTION 19

You are working with a deaf student, Sarah, who uses a cochlear implant for hearing. Sarah is struggling with speech and language development. What intervention should you consider to address Sarah's speech and language challenges effectively?

    A. Encourage Sarah to rely solely on sign language for communication.
    B. Provide speech therapy with a focus on auditory and oral skills.
    C. Suggest a switch to a specialized school for deaf students.
    D. Advise Sarah to communicate exclusively in writing.

Answer:

QUESTION 20

You are a special education teacher working with a deaf student, Alex, who excels in mathematics but struggles with English language arts. How can you support Alex's learning in English language arts while building on his strengths in math?

    A. Advise Alex to focus exclusively on mathematics and abandon English language arts.
    B. Provide additional support in English language arts, such as tutoring or speech therapy.
    C. Encourage Alex to use sign language for all subjects to improve communication.
    D. Recommend that Alex switch to a specialized school for students with math-related strengths.

Answer:

QUESTION 21

You are working with a group of deaf and hard of hearing students in a mainstream school. They are preparing for a science fair presentation. How can you ensure that the presentation is accessible and inclusive for all students, regardless of their hearing status?

    A. Require all students to use spoken language only during the presentation.
    B. Encourage students to use multimedia presentations with visual aids.
    C. Advise students to present individually to avoid communication challenges.
    D. Recommend canceling the presentation due to communication barriers.

Answer:

QUESTION 22

You are working with a group of deaf and hard of hearing students, and you want to promote cognitive development through multisensory instruction. Which teaching strategy is most likely to enhance their cognitive growth?

    A. Exclusively using written materials for instruction.
    B. Incorporating a variety of sensory experiences into lessons.
    C. Isolating each sense to focus on one at a time.
    D. Advancing students to higher-grade content quickly.

Answer:

QUESTION 23

You are working with a young deaf student who is struggling with cognitive development. What research-based intervention should you consider to promote cognitive growth in this student?

- A. Encourage the use of sign language exclusively for communication.
- B. Provide regular exposure to age-appropriate auditory experiences.
- C. Advise the student to focus solely on visual learning materials.
- D. Recommend repeating the same instructional methods.

Answer:

QUESTION 24

You are working with a group of deaf and hard of hearing students who are struggling with language and cognition. What instructional approach is likely to have the greatest impact on their development?

- A. Focusing solely on visual and written materials.
- B. Encouraging students to rely solely on lip-reading.
- C. Incorporating sign language into lessons.
- D. Advancing students to higher-grade content quickly.

Answer:

QUESTION 25

You are working with a deaf high school student who is interested in a career in mathematics. What sensory input strategies can you employ to support their cognitive development in this subject?

- A. Advise the student to rely solely on written materials for learning math.
- B. Provide tactile and visual aids to enhance understanding of mathematical concepts.
- C. Encourage the student to focus on auditory explanations of math problems.
- D. Recommend skipping advanced math courses due to communication challenges.

Answer:

QUESTION 26

You are conducting research on the cognitive development of children who are deaf or hard of hearing. What aspect of sensory input should you focus on to better understand its impact on cognition in this population?

- A. The exclusion of sensory input in educational settings.
- B. The use of sign language as the primary mode of communication.
- C. The incorporation of visual, spatial, and tactile sensory input.
- D. Advancing students to higher-grade content quickly.

Answer:

QUESTION 27

You are a special education teacher working with a group of deaf and hard of hearing students. One student is struggling with language acquisition and cognitive development. What instructional approach should you consider to support this student's cognitive growth effectively?

- A. Isolate the student from the group to minimize distractions.
- B. Provide instruction exclusively through auditory means.
- C. Incorporate visual and tactile learning experiences.
- D. Recommend advancing the student to a higher grade level.

Answer:

QUESTION 28

You are a special education teacher working with a group of deaf and hard of hearing students in a mainstream school. One of your students, Emily, is experiencing challenges in cognitive development and language acquisition. She primarily relies on lip-reading and written materials for communication. Emily's parents are concerned about her progress. How can you address Emily's needs effectively to promote her cognitive development?

    A. Recommend Emily focus solely on lip-reading for communication.
    B. Encourage Emily to advance to a higher-grade level to challenge her.
    C. Incorporate tactile and visual aids into lessons to support her learning.
    D. Suggest transferring Emily to a specialized school for deaf students.

Answer:

QUESTION 29

You are working with a group of deaf and hard of hearing students, and one of your students, Sam, has a cochlear implant. Despite the implant, Sam still faces challenges in language and cognitive development. You want to design an effective intervention plan for Sam. What approach should you consider to address Sam's needs?

    A. Encourage Sam to rely solely on the cochlear implant for auditory input.
    B. Provide written materials exclusively for Sam's learning.
    C. Incorporate auditory experiences into lessons, complementing the implant.
    D. Recommend switching Sam to a school exclusively for students with cochlear implants.

Answer:

QUESTION 30

You are conducting research on the cognitive development of a group of deaf and hard of hearing children. Your study involves assessing the impact of sensory input on their cognitive growth. After analyzing the data, you find that children who received multisensory instruction outperformed those who received unisensory instruction. What conclusion can you draw from this research finding?

    A. Multisensory instruction has no significant impact on cognitive development.
    B. Deaf and hard of hearing children perform better with unisensory instruction.
    C. Multisensory instruction positively influences cognitive development in this population.
    D. The research findings are inconclusive and require further investigation.

Answer:

QUESTION 31

You are a special education teacher working with a group of deaf and hard of hearing students in a mainstream school. You suspect that one of your students, Sarah, may have additional learning disabilities in addition to her hearing impairment. What should be your initial step in the screening and referral process for Sarah?

    A. Immediately request a formal assessment for learning disabilities.
    B. Consult with Sarah's parents to gather additional information.
    C. Assume that Sarah's hearing impairment is the sole reason for her difficulties.
    D. Wait until the end of the school year to assess her progress.

Answer:

QUESTION 32

You are a special education teacher working with a deaf student named Alex in a mainstream elementary school. Alex's parents are concerned about his academic progress and believe he may need specialized services. What is the appropriate next step in the referral and classification process for Alex?

    A.   Request an immediate referral for special education services.
    B.   Collaborate with the school's Child Study Team to assess Alex's needs.
    C.   Advise the parents to explore private tutoring options.
    D.   Dismiss the parents' concerns as typical for deaf students.

Answer:

QUESTION 33

You are a special education teacher working with a group of deaf and hard of hearing students. As part of the screening process, you administer a standardized assessment to a student named Jake. Jake's performance on the assessment is significantly lower than expected based on his age and grade level. What should you do next?

    A.   Recommend that Jake be placed in a special education class immediately.
    B.   Consult with colleagues to determine if the assessment was administered correctly.
    C.   Ignore the assessment results as they may not be accurate for deaf students.
    D.   Advise Jake to repeat the grade to catch up academically.

Answer:

QUESTION 34

You are a special education teacher working with a deaf high school student named Mia. Mia is preparing for a standardized state assessment in mathematics. She uses sign language as her primary mode of communication. What is the most appropriate way to modify or adapt the assessment to accommodate Mia's needs?

    A.   Provide an interpreter to sign the assessment s to Mia.
    B.   Administer the assessment in written form only.
    C.   Exclude Mia from taking the assessment due to her communication mode.
    D.   Offer Mia extra time to complete the assessment.

Answer:

QUESTION 35

You are a special education teacher working with a group of deaf and hard of hearing students who are preparing for a standardized reading assessment. Some of your students use sign language, while others rely on lip-reading. What is the most appropriate way to modify the assessment to ensure fair and accurate results for all students?

    A.   Administer the assessment in a written format only.
    B.   Provide a sign language interpreter for all students.
    C.   Offer lip-reading support during the assessment.
    D.   Individualize assessment modifications based on each student's needs.

Answer:

QUESTION 36

You are a special education teacher working with a group of deaf and hard of hearing students preparing for a standardized national assessment. One of your students, Ben, has additional disabilities that impact his motor skills. What is the most appropriate assessment modification to ensure Ben can participate effectively in the assessment?

    A. Exclude Ben from taking the assessment due to his motor difficulties.
    B. Provide a scribe or assistive technology for Ben to record his responses.
    C. Advise Ben to take the assessment orally instead of in written form.
    D. Administer a different, less challenging assessment to Ben.

Answer:

QUESTION 37

You are a special education teacher working with a deaf student named Jordan who uses American Sign Language (ASL) as their primary mode of communication. After conducting an ASL assessment, you discover that Jordan exhibits advanced proficiency in ASL morphology, but struggles with ASL syntax. What should be your next step to support Jordan's ASL development?

    A. Focus solely on advanced morphology exercises to reinforce their strengths.
    B. Create individualized lessons that target their specific syntax difficulties.
    C. Recommend switching to a different communication mode.
    D. Exclude syntax assessments due to Jordan's struggles.

Answer:

QUESTION 38

You have conducted an ASL assessment for a group of deaf and hard of hearing students. One student, Maya, exhibits significant variability in their ASL proficiency, excelling in semantics but struggling with pragmatics. How should you communicate these assessment results to Maya and her parents effectively?

    A. Provide a detailed report highlighting Maya's difficulties and recommend additional support.
    B. Share only the positive aspects of Maya's performance to boost her confidence.
    C. Exclude the results related to pragmatics to avoid causing concern.
    D. Advise Maya's parents to seek external ASL instruction for her.

Answer:

QUESTION 39

You have assessed a deaf student's ASL skills and found that they have strong semantics but significant difficulties with ASL morphology. As a special education teacher, what should be your primary goal in communicating these assessment results to the student?

    A. Encourage the student to focus solely on semantics and ignore morphology.
    B. Help the student understand the importance of balanced ASL development.
    C. Suggest switching to a different communication mode to overcome difficulties.
    D. Advise the student to rely solely on assistive technology for communication.

Answer:

QUESTION 40

You have conducted an ASL assessment for a group of deaf students, and the results indicate varying levels of proficiency in ASL syntax. How can you effectively communicate these assessment results to the students and encourage their growth in this area?

    A.   Group all students together and provide general feedback about syntax.
    B.   Discuss individual assessment results privately to avoid embarrassment.
    C.   Exclude the assessment results related to syntax to prevent discouragement.
    D.   Organize group workshops focusing on ASL syntax improvement.

Answer:

QUESTION 41

You have conducted an ASL assessment for a deaf student, Leo, who struggles with both syntax and pragmatics. Leo's parents are concerned about his ASL development. How should you communicate these assessment results to Leo's parents to foster a constructive partnership in addressing Leo's needs?

    A.   Downplay Leo's difficulties to avoid causing concern.
    B.   Share only Leo's strengths to maintain a positive outlook.
    C.   Provide a clear and honest overview of Leo's challenges and strengths.
    D.   Advise Leo's parents to switch to a different communication mode.

Answer:

QUESTION 42

You have assessed a group of deaf and hard of hearing students' ASL proficiency, and the results show a general need for improvement in semantics across the group. What strategy should you employ to communicate these assessment results to students and facilitate their development in ASL semantics?

    A.   Exclude the assessment results to avoid discouraging the students.
    B.   Organize one-on-one sessions with each student to discuss their needs.
    C.   Conduct group seminars on ASL semantics to address the common challenge.
    D.   Recommend that students rely solely on written communication.

Answer:

QUESTION 43

You are a special education teacher working with a deaf student named Alex who has additional disabilities. You are tasked with developing an Individualized Education Plan (IEP) that includes a Communication Plan. What should be the primary consideration when creating a Communication Plan for Alex?

    A.   Prioritize sign language as the sole mode of communication.
    B.   Focus on spoken language to align with general education standards.
    C.   Tailor the plan to Alex's unique needs and communication preferences.
    D.   Implement a standardized Communication Plan for all students with disabilities.

Answer:

QUESTION 44

You are a special education teacher working with a group of deaf and hard of hearing students in a mainstream school. You are responsible for aligning their learning goals with national, state, and local content and performance standards. What should be your primary focus when creating learning goals for these students?

A. Adapt the standards to match the students' abilities.
B. Align the learning goals with the general education curriculum.
C. Disregard the standards and focus solely on individual needs.
D. Develop goals that are unrelated to the established standards.

Answer:

QUESTION 45

You are a special education teacher working with a deaf student, Mia, who has additional disabilities. When developing Mia's Communication Plan, what key factor should you consider to make it effective?

A. Implement a standardized Communication Plan used for all students with disabilities.
B. Prioritize the use of written communication to ensure clarity.
C. Tailor the plan to Mia's unique needs, abilities, and communication preferences.
D. Focus exclusively on sign language as the primary mode of communication.

Answer:

QUESTION 46

You are working with a group of deaf and hard of hearing students in a mainstream school, and your goal is to create individualized learning goals that align with the general education curriculum. What is the most critical consideration when sequencing these goals for your students?

A. Ensuring that all students progress at the same pace to meet grade-level standards.
B. Adapting the general education curriculum to match the students' abilities.
C. Using standardized goals for all students to maintain consistency.
D. Aligning the sequence of goals with each student's specific learning needs and abilities.

Answer:

QUESTION 47

You are a special education teacher working with a group of deaf and hard of hearing students, each with different levels of proficiency in sign language. What is the most effective approach to developing Communication Plans that meet the diverse needs of your students?

A. Enforce the use of sign language as the sole mode of communication.
B. Provide individualized Communication Plans based on each student's sign language proficiency.
C. Develop a standardized Communication Plan for all students to maintain consistency.
D. Discourage the use of sign language to encourage spoken communication.

Answer:

QUESTION 48

You are a special education teacher working with a deaf student, Ben, who has a unique set of learning needs. When setting long-term individualized learning goals for Ben, what should be your primary focus?

A. Aligning the goals with general education standards regardless of his abilities.
B. Adapting the goals to suit Ben's preferences exclusively.
C. Ensuring that the goals are consistent with Ben's specific learning needs and abilities.
D. Creating goals that are unrelated to the general education curriculum.

Answer:

QUESTION 49

You are a special education teacher working with a deaf student named Sarah who is struggling in her general education math class. Sarah uses sign language as her primary mode of communication. What is the most likely challenge Sarah is facing in her math class due to her deafness, and how can you address it effectively?

- A. Sarah may have difficulty understanding spoken math concepts. You can provide sign language support and visual aids to enhance comprehension.
- B. Sarah may struggle with physical education activities. You can assign alternative assignments related to math concepts.
- C. Sarah's deafness may result in social isolation in the math class. You can encourage peer interaction to build social connections.
- D. Sarah may have trouble reading math textbooks. You can recommend switching to audio versions.

Answer:

QUESTION 50

You are a special education teacher working with a group of deaf and hard of hearing students in a mainstream high school. Some students use sign language, while others rely on lip-reading. How can you plan instruction that effectively caters to the diverse communication needs of these students in a history class?

- A. Implement a single teaching method that suits the majority of students.
- B. Provide written materials exclusively for all students.
- C. Offer both sign language interpretation and written materials as options.
- D. Recommend that students with lip-reading skills teach their peers.

Answer:

QUESTION 51

You are a special education teacher working with a group of deaf and hard of hearing students who have varying degrees of hearing loss. How should you approach instruction in a science class to accommodate the different levels of hearing loss among your students effectively?

- A. Use spoken language and adjust your volume based on each student's hearing loss level.
- B. Focus exclusively on visual demonstrations to ensure understanding.
- C. Provide written materials and sign language support as needed.
- D. Advise students with severe hearing loss to rely solely on written materials.

Answer:

QUESTION 52

You are a special education teacher working with a deaf student, David, in a general education literature class. David is struggling with comprehending complex literary texts. What instructional strategy can you employ to address his difficulties effectively?

- A. Focus exclusively on written language instruction.
- B. Provide sign language support and visual aids to enhance comprehension.
- C. Assign simpler texts to accommodate David's needs.
- D. Advise David to use assistive technology for reading.

Answer:

QUESTION 53

You are a special education teacher working with a group of deaf and hard of hearing students in a physical education class. Some students use sign language, while others rely on lip-reading. How can you plan physical education activities that cater to the diverse communication needs of these students effectively?

    A.   Assign written assignments related to physical education concepts.
    B.   Implement activities that do not require communication.
    C.   Offer both sign language interpretation and visual cues during activities.
    D.   Recommend students with lip-reading skills lead the activities.

Answer:

QUESTION 54

You are a special education teacher working with a deaf student, Emily, in a general education geography class. Emily is having difficulty understanding spoken content during class lectures. What instructional strategy can you employ to support Emily's learning effectively?

    A.   Advise Emily to rely solely on written materials for studying.
    B.   Provide sign language interpretation during class lectures.
    C.   Assign a peer note-taker to transcribe lectures for Emily.
    D.   Recommend that Emily use audio recordings to review lectures.

Answer:

QUESTION 55

You are a special education teacher working with a deaf student named Liam who uses American Sign Language (ASL) as his primary mode of communication. After conducting a literacy assessment, you find that Liam is struggling with reading comprehension. What is the most effective strategy for interpreting these assessment results and planning instruction for Liam?

    A.   Recommend speech therapy to improve his spoken language skills.
    B.   Provide sign language support and visual aids to enhance reading comprehension.
    C.   Focus solely on written language instruction to address the issue.
    D.   Suggest that Liam switch to a different communication mode.

Answer:

QUESTION 56

You are a special education teacher working with a group of deaf and hard of hearing students in a general education classroom. Some students use spoken language, while others rely on sign language. What instructional strategy can you employ to effectively teach vocabulary to these diverse learners?

    A.   Focus exclusively on spoken language instruction.
    B.   Implement sign language instruction for all students.
    C.   Offer both spoken and sign language instruction as options.
    D.   Assign written vocabulary assignments for all students.

Answer:

QUESTION 57

You are a special education teacher working with a deaf student, Ava, who uses spoken language and cochlear implants. Ava has difficulty with phonological awareness. What evidence-based strategy can you employ to help Ava develop her phonological awareness skills effectively?

    A.   Focus solely on visual aids and sign language to address the issue.
    B.   Recommend that Ava rely solely on written language for instruction.
    C.   Provide explicit instruction in speech sounds and phonological awareness.
    D.   Suggest switching to a different communication mode.

Answer:

QUESTION 58

You are a special education teacher working with a deaf student, Owen, who primarily uses sign language for communication. Owen is struggling with written language skills. What evidence-based strategy can you employ to help Owen develop his written language skills effectively?

    A.   Recommend speech therapy to improve his spoken language skills.
    B.   Provide sign language interpretation for all written materials.
    C.   Offer explicit instruction in written language skills and composition.
    D.   Suggest that Owen switch to spoken language as the primary mode of communication.

Answer:

QUESTION 59

You are a special education teacher working with a group of deaf and hard of hearing students in a reading class. Some students use spoken language, while others rely on sign language. What is the most effective approach to teaching reading comprehension to cater to the diverse communication needs of these students?

    A.   Provide sign language interpretation for all reading materials.
    B.   Implement spoken language instruction for all students.
    C.   Offer both sign language interpretation and visual aids as options.
    D.   Assign written reading comprehension assignments for all students.

Answer:

QUESTION 60

You are a special education teacher working with a deaf student named Maya who uses a combination of spoken language and sign language. Maya is struggling with language development. What evidence-based strategy can you employ to support Maya's language development effectively?

    A.   Focus exclusively on sign language instruction.
    B.   Recommend that Maya rely solely on written language for communication.
    C.   Provide a balanced approach, combining spoken and sign language instruction.
    D.   Suggest switching to a different communication mode.

Answer:

QUESTION 61

You have a deaf student, Emily, who is actively involved in her school's drama club. She enjoys participating in school plays and community theater productions. How can you facilitate effective communication for Emily during her drama club activities, which often involve group rehearsals and performances?

    A.   Advise Emily to rely solely on written communication with her peers.
    B.   Provide sign language interpreters for all drama club activities.
    C.   Encourage Emily to teach her peers basic sign language for essential communication.
    D.   Implement a combination of sign language interpreters and visual cues during rehearsals and performances.

Answer:

QUESTION 62

You are a special education teacher working with a group of deaf and hard of hearing students who are preparing for a field trip to a local museum. The museum is known for its interactive exhibits and engaging programs. What communication strategy should you employ to ensure that these students can fully participate and benefit from the museum visit?

    A.   Assign written assignments related to the museum exhibits.
    B.   Provide sign language interpreters for the entire field trip.
    C.   Offer visual aids and written materials to enhance understanding.
    D.   Encourage students to rely solely on lip-reading skills during the visit.

Answer:

QUESTION 63

You are planning a community service project for your deaf and hard of hearing students to engage with local organizations. One of the activities involves volunteering at a community garden. How can you support effective communication between your students and the community members during this project?

    A.   Assign written communication tasks for all interactions.
    B.   Provide sign language interpreters for the entire community service project.
    C.   Encourage students to teach basic sign language signs related to gardening.
    D.   Implement a combination of sign language interpreters and visual cues during interactions.

Answer:

QUESTION 64

You are a special education teacher working with a group of deaf and hard of hearing students who are participating in a science fair at a local convention center. How can you ensure effective communication for your students during this event, which involves various presentations and discussions?

    A.   Recommend that students rely solely on written communication for interactions.
    B.   Provide sign language interpreters for specific presentations and discussions.
    C.   Encourage students to use assistive technology for all communication.
    D.   Implement a combination of sign language interpreters and written materials for interactions.

Answer:

QUESTION 65

You are a special education teacher working with a group of deaf and hard of hearing students who are taking part in a community cleanup initiative in a local park. How can you facilitate effective communication between your students and other volunteers during this outdoor activity?

    A.   Assign written instructions for all tasks.
    B.   Provide sign language interpreters for the entire cleanup initiative.
    C.   Encourage students to use lip-reading skills exclusively.
    D.   Implement a combination of visual cues and sign language interpreters during the activity.

Answer:

QUESTION 66

You are organizing a workshop on financial literacy for a group of deaf and hard of hearing students in collaboration with a local bank. The workshop will cover topics such as budgeting, saving, and financial planning. How can you support effective communication between the bank representatives and your students during the workshop?

A. Provide written materials and assignments for all workshop activities.
B. Assign sign language interpreters for the entire duration of the workshop.
C. Encourage students to rely solely on lip-reading skills during the workshop.
D. Implement a combination of sign language interpreters and visual aids for the workshop.

Answer:

QUESTION 67

You are planning a lesson on American Deaf Culture for your students who are deaf and hard of hearing. You want to emphasize the importance of Deaf history. What approach would be most effective for fostering a deep understanding of Deaf history and culture?

A. Assign a research project on prominent historical Deaf figures.
B. Invite a Deaf guest speaker to share personal experiences.
C. Provide written materials exclusively for students to read.
D. Encourage students to solely rely on lip-reading skills for communication.

Answer:

QUESTION 68

You are a special education teacher working with a group of deaf and hard of hearing students who are preparing for a cultural exchange event with a Deaf community. What strategy would be most effective in preparing your students for meaningful interactions during the exchange?

A. Provide written guidelines for appropriate behavior.
B. Assign lip-reading practice as the primary communication skill.
C. Offer cultural sensitivity training and basic sign language instruction.
D. Encourage students to use written communication exclusively.

Answer:

QUESTION 69

You are organizing a school assembly to celebrate Deaf History Month. How can you ensure that the assembly is inclusive and respectful of Deaf culture and heritage?

A. Display written information about Deaf history on screens.
B. Play recorded speeches of prominent Deaf figures.
C. Invite Deaf individuals to perform sign language poetry.
D. Encourage students to rely solely on lip-reading during the assembly.

Answer:

QUESTION 70

You are planning a field trip for your deaf and hard of hearing students to visit a local Deaf cultural center. What key element should be incorporated into the field trip to promote meaningful interactions and cultural understanding?

A. Providing written brochures about Deaf culture at the center.
B. Assigning individual reading assignments about Deaf history.
C. Arranging guided tours led by Deaf cultural center staff.
D. Encouraging students to rely solely on written notes for communication.

Answer:

QUESTION 71

You are a special education teacher working with a group of deaf and hard of hearing students who are interested in participating in a community event organized by a Deaf organization. How can you facilitate their involvement and interaction with the Deaf community effectively?

A. Provide written instructions for students to follow during the event.
B. Encourage students to rely solely on lip-reading skills for communication.
C. Arrange for sign language interpreters to be present throughout the event.
D. Assign individual research projects about the Deaf organization.

Answer:

QUESTION 72

You are organizing a community awareness event to promote interaction with individuals who are deaf or hard of hearing. What should be a central focus of this event to encourage meaningful interactions and mutual understanding?

A. Providing written materials about the challenges faced by the Deaf community.
B. Offering a sign language workshop for participants.
C. Assigning students to practice lip-reading with community members.
D. Encouraging participants to communicate solely through written notes.

Answer:

QUESTION 73

You are a special education teacher working with a deaf student named Ethan, and you want to ensure his successful inclusion in extracurricular activities. What is the most effective strategy to collaborate with professionals and community agencies to promote Ethan's participation in these activities?

A. Send written information about Ethan's needs to relevant professionals.
B. Encourage Ethan to communicate directly with community agencies.
C. Schedule meetings with professionals to discuss Ethan's needs and accommodations.
D. Advise Ethan to handle all communication independently.

Answer:

QUESTION 74

You have organized a collaborative event involving deaf and hard of hearing students, general education teachers, and local community agencies. How should you evaluate the effectiveness of this collaborative activity?

A. Provide a written survey for participants to fill out anonymously.
B. Rely on anecdotal feedback from a few participants.
C. Assign a written reflection task to all participants.
D. Conduct one-on-one interviews with a select group of participants.

Answer:

QUESTION 75

You are a special education teacher working with a group of deaf and hard of hearing students, and you need to communicate with a speech therapist about a student's progress. What is the most effective strategy for communicating with the speech therapist about the student's characteristics and needs?

A. Provide a written report with detailed information about the student.
B. Encourage the student to communicate directly with the speech therapist.
C. Schedule a meeting with the speech therapist and the student.
D. Advise the student to handle all communication independently.

Answer:

QUESTION 76

You are collaborating with a community agency to organize a career workshop for deaf and hard of hearing students. What strategy would be most effective in evaluating the success of this collaborative activity?

A. Rely on feedback from a few students who attended the workshop.
B. Conduct individual interviews with students who participated.
C. Distribute a written survey to all students who attended anonymously.
D. Encourage students to provide verbal feedback during the workshop.

Answer:

QUESTION 77

You are collaborating with a local healthcare agency to support the medical needs of a deaf student named Mia. What is the most effective strategy for communicating with healthcare professionals about Mia's characteristics and needs?

A. Advise Mia to communicate directly with healthcare professionals.
B. Schedule meetings with healthcare professionals to discuss Mia's needs.
C. Provide a brief written summary of Mia's characteristics.
D. Encourage healthcare professionals to contact Mia independently.

Answer:

QUESTION 78

You are organizing a collaborative event involving deaf and hard of hearing students, their families, and community agencies. What is the most effective way to evaluate the success of this collaborative activity?

A. Conduct one-on-one interviews with a few participants.
B. Encourage participants to provide verbal feedback during the event.
C. Assign written reflections to all participants.
D. Provide a written survey for all participants to complete anonymously.

Answer:

QUESTION 79

You are a special education teacher working with deaf and hard of hearing students, and you want to ensure you uphold high standards for professional practice. What is the most effective way to participate in professional activities that benefit your students?

A. Attend occasional workshops on general education practices.
B. Join a professional organization dedicated to deaf education.
C. Engage in personal research without external involvement.
D. Encourage students to independently seek resources.

Answer:

QUESTION 80

You are a special education teacher working with deaf and hard of hearing students. You want to stay updated on the latest research and best practices in the field. What is the most effective strategy to enhance your professional knowledge and engage in lifelong professional growth and development?

A. Rely on the school's curriculum without seeking external resources.
B. Attend occasional seminars on general education topics.
C. Subscribe to deaf education journals and participate in webinars.
D. Encourage students to independently research and provide feedback.

Answer:

QUESTION 81

You are a special education teacher committed to upholding high standards for professional practice in the education of deaf and hard of hearing students. What action demonstrates your commitment to this principle?

A. Isolating yourself from professional networks and resources.
B. Occasional attendance at general education conferences.
C. Active participation in a national deaf education association.
D. Encouraging students to independently manage their education.

Answer:

QUESTION 82

You are a special education teacher focused on professional growth and development while working with deaf and hard of hearing students. What resource is most likely to provide you with the latest evidence-based practices and strategies in the field?

A. Isolated personal research without external involvement.
B. Occasional attendance at general education workshops.
C. Membership in a deaf education professional association.
D. Encouraging students to independently access resources.

Answer:

QUESTION 83

You are a special education teacher dedicated to upholding high standards for professional practice in the education of deaf and hard of hearing students. What activity aligns best with this commitment?

A. Attending sporadic conferences unrelated to your field.
B. Engaging in personal research unrelated to education.
C. Active participation in a national association for deaf educators.
D. Encouraging students to independently manage their education.

Answer:

QUESTION 84

You are a special education teacher who values continuous professional growth while working with deaf and hard of hearing students. What resource is most likely to provide you with ongoing support and opportunities for professional development?

A. Relying solely on classroom experiences without external involvement.
B. Attending occasional general education conferences.
C. Membership in a local special education association.
D. Subscription to a deaf education journal and participation in online courses.

Answer:

QUESTION 85

You are a special education teacher working with a deaf student who comes from a culturally diverse background. The student's primary language is American Sign Language (ASL), and their family primarily communicates in ASL at home. The school primarily uses English as the language of instruction. The student is struggling with reading comprehension in English. Which strategy is most appropriate for addressing this situation?

A. Providing additional English reading materials for the student.
B. Encouraging the student to speak more in English during class.
C. Collaborating with the student's family to incorporate ASL into English reading lessons.
D. Assigning extra homework in English reading comprehension.

Answer:

QUESTION 86

You are a special education teacher working with a hard of hearing student in a mainstream classroom. The student uses hearing aids to assist with hearing but still faces challenges in understanding spoken instructions. Which accommodation is most suitable to address this issue?

    A.   Providing written instructions for all assignments.
    B.   Assigning a sign language interpreter for all classes.
    C.   Increasing the volume of classroom speakers.
    D.   Encouraging the student to rely solely on their hearing aids.

Answer:

QUESTION 87

You have a deaf student who struggles with social interactions in the classroom. The student often feels isolated due to communication barriers. Which strategy would be most effective in promoting social inclusion for this student?

    A.   Encouraging the student to interact more with hearing classmates.
    B.   Providing peer buddies who know sign language to assist the student.
    C.   Isolating the student in a separate room for one-on-one instruction.
    D.   Discouraging the use of sign language to encourage lip reading.

Answer:

QUESTION 88

You are a special education teacher working with a deaf student who is bilingual, using both American Sign Language (ASL) and English. The student often struggles with expressing themselves in written English. What approach is most effective in supporting the student's language development in English?

    A.   Focusing exclusively on improving the student's ASL skills.
    B.   Encouraging the student to communicate solely in ASL.
    C.   Providing targeted English language tutoring and practice.
    D.   Discouraging the use of ASL to avoid confusion.

Answer:

QUESTION 89

You are a special education teacher working with a culturally diverse group of deaf students, each with different primary languages and communication preferences. One student primarily uses American Sign Language (ASL), while another primarily uses a visual communication system. You need to plan a group activity to promote social interaction and collaboration among these students. What is the most inclusive approach to designing this activity?

    A.   Conduct the activity in English to ensure equal participation.
    B.   Create two separate activities, one in ASL and one in the visual communication system.
    C.   Facilitate the activity in a way that allows students to choose their preferred communication method.
    D.   Assign a sign language interpreter to facilitate communication during the activity.

Answer:

QUESTION 90

You have a deaf student from a culturally diverse background who is struggling with understanding complex written texts in English. The student's first language is a sign language that is different from American Sign Language (ASL). What would be the most effective strategy to support this student's reading comprehension skills?

    A. Provide additional English reading materials with no ASL support.
    B. Encourage the student to rely solely on ASL for reading comprehension.
    C. Collaborate with the student's family to incorporate their sign language into English reading lessons.
    D. Assign more homework in English reading comprehension to practice.

Answer:

QUESTION 91

You have a hard of hearing student who is part of a culturally diverse classroom. The student uses hearing aids but still struggles with following classroom discussions due to background noise and various accents among classmates. What accommodation would be most appropriate to help the student succeed in this inclusive environment?

    A. Providing the student with a noise-canceling headset.
    B. Encouraging the student to request repetitions during discussions.
    C. Assigning the student a sign language interpreter for all classes.
    D. Isolating the student in a separate quiet room for instruction.

Answer:

QUESTION 92

A 5-year-old child with profound hearing loss has been receiving auditory-oral therapy to develop speech and language skills. Despite consistent therapy, the child's speech remains difficult to understand, and they frequently mispronounce words. What should the special education teacher consider as the most likely factor contributing to the child's speech difficulties?

    A. Lack of motivation to improve speech skills.
    B. An underlying cognitive impairment.
    C. Insufficient therapy sessions.
    D. Limited access to auditory input.

Answer:

QUESTION 93

A 7-year-old deaf student who uses sign language as their primary mode of communication is integrated into a mainstream classroom. The teacher notices that the student is excelling in reading and writing but struggles with expressive spoken language. What is the most likely reason for this disparity in language skills?

    A. Lack of effort in improving spoken language skills.
    B. Inadequate support for sign language communication in the classroom.
    C. An underlying cognitive impairment.
    D. A focus on reading and writing at home.

Answer:

QUESTION 94

You are working with a group of students who have varying degrees of hearing loss. One student has mild hearing loss, while another has profound hearing loss. Which of the following speech development characteristics is likely to be common among both students?

A. Precise articulation and clear speech.
B. Limited vocabulary and communication skills.
C. Delayed speech and language milestones.
D. High-pitched and hypernasal speech.

Answer:

QUESTION 95

A 10-year-old deaf student who uses cochlear implants for hearing participates in a school play. During the play, the student struggles with articulating their lines clearly, and some words are difficult to understand. What should be the teacher's primary consideration when supporting this student's speech development in this context?

A. Increasing the volume of the cochlear implants.
B. Providing additional speech therapy sessions.
C. Encouraging the use of sign language during the play.
D. Using visual supports and clear enunciation during rehearsals.

Answer:

QUESTION 96

You are working with a group of students who are deaf or hard of hearing in a classroom. One student has a cochlear implant, while another uses a hearing aid. Despite using these devices, they both exhibit difficulty in discriminating speech sounds. What is the most likely factor contributing to their difficulty?

A. Lack of motivation to improve listening skills.
B. Insufficiently advanced hearing technologies.
C. Inadequate exposure to spoken language.
D. Underlying cognitive deficits.

Answer:

QUESTION 97

You are working with a group of deaf students who have diverse learning styles. One student is a visual learner, another is tactile, and a third is auditory. How can you best support these students' diverse learning styles to enhance their cognitive development?

A. Use a single teaching approach that accommodates all learning styles simultaneously.
B. Create individualized learning plans based on each student's learning style.
C. Focus solely on auditory learning methods to ensure consistency.
D. Implement a strict visual learning approach for all students.

Answer:

QUESTION 98

You have a student who is deaf and primarily a visual learner. However, they struggle with reading comprehension. Which approach would be most effective in supporting this student's development in this area?

A. Providing written materials with complex visual graphics.
B. Offering video-based learning materials without text.
C. Incorporating visual aids alongside text-based materials.
D. Assigning additional reading assignments to improve skills.

Answer:

QUESTION 99

You have a deaf student who excels in spatial learning and problem-solving. How can you leverage their spatial learning style to enhance their cognitive development in a classroom setting?

    A. Encourage them to rely solely on sign language for communication.
    B. Provide hands-on activities and manipulatives for learning.
    C. Assign auditory-heavy tasks to challenge their learning style.
    D. Focus on rote memorization to improve their cognitive skills.

Answer:

QUESTION 100

You have a hard of hearing student who struggles with socialization and forming peer relationships in a mainstream classroom. How can you help improve their social development?

    A. Encourage the student to spend more time alone to avoid social difficulties.
    B. Provide opportunities for group activities that emphasize their preferred learning style.
    C. Isolate the student in a separate room for one-on-one instruction.
    D. Discourage the use of sign language to encourage lip reading.

Answer:

QUESTION 101

Javier is an 11-year-old student who is deaf and comes from a culturally and linguistically diverse background. He primarily uses spoken English and has a cochlear implant. Javier's recent assessments indicate that he excels in social studies but requires additional support in mathematics. Considering Javier's assessment results and background, what recommendations might you make for his educational program, placement, and services?

    A. Advocate for a mainstream classroom placement with appropriate supports for his hearing impairment and provide additional support in mathematics while offering advanced coursework in social studies.
    B. Suggest placement in a specialized program exclusively focused on auditory training to improve his mathematics skills.
    C. Propose a self-contained classroom for students with hearing impairments without additional services in social studies.
    D. Recommend placement in a general education classroom without additional supports.

Answer:

QUESTION 102

Emma is a 10-year-old student who is deaf. She has recently transitioned from a self-contained classroom to a mainstream classroom with appropriate supports. Emma is struggling to effectively communicate with her hearing peers, and some of her classmates are finding it challenging to interact with her. What technique would be most effective in supporting Emma's meaningful integration into the mainstream classroom?

    A. Facilitating structured peer interactions that promote effective communication between Emma and her classmates.
    B. Encouraging Emma to rely solely on sign language to foster independence in communication.
    C. Suggesting that Emma only interact with other students who are deaf or hard of hearing.
    D. Advocating for Emma's return to a self-contained classroom for students with hearing impairments.

Answer:

QUESTION 103

Jacob is a 12-year-old student who is hard of hearing. He occasionally displays disruptive behavior in the classroom, which may be related to his frustration with communication difficulties. What behavior-management strategy would be most appropriate for helping Jacob establish and maintain socially acceptable behavior in the learning environment?

    A. Implementing a system of visual cues or signals to communicate expectations and provide positive reinforcement for appropriate behavior.
    B. Isolating Jacob from the rest of the class to prevent disruptive behavior.
    C. Enforcing strict disciplinary measures to discourage disruptive behavior.
    D. Ignoring Jacob's disruptive behavior to avoid reinforcing it with attention.

Answer:

QUESTION 104

Sarah is a 15-year-old student who is deaf. She has a reserved personality and often struggles to connect with her teachers and peers. What effective strategy could a teacher employ to establish and maintain rapport with Sarah?

    A. Creating opportunities for one-on-one interactions and actively listening to Sarah's thoughts and concerns.
    B. Assuming that Sarah prefers to be left alone due to her reserved personality.
    C. Encouraging Sarah to participate in group activities to help her become more outgoing.
    D. Avoiding direct communication with Sarah to respect her personal space.

Answer:

QUESTION 105

Elena is an 8-year-old student who is deaf and has recently been placed in a mainstream classroom with appropriate supports. She is struggling to follow classroom routines and expectations. What technique might be most effective in helping Elena adapt to the classroom environment?

    A. Providing visual schedules and cues to help Elena anticipate and navigate daily routines.
    B. Assigning additional homework to reinforce classroom expectations.
    C. Requesting a one-on-one aide for Elena at all times.
    D. Excluding Elena from classroom activities to minimize disruptions.

Answer:

QUESTION 106

Mark is a 16-year-old student who is hard of hearing and has a strong interest in technology. He occasionally becomes frustrated when he faces communication barriers in the classroom. What behavior-management technique might be most effective in helping Mark cope with communication challenges?

    A. Encouraging Mark to use assistive technology tools that facilitate communication in the classroom.
    B. Issuing strict consequences for any display of frustration or disruptive behavior.
    C. Ignoring Mark's frustration to avoid reinforcing it with attention.
    D. Excluding Mark from group activities to minimize disruptions.

Answer:

QUESTION 107

James is a 14-year-old student who is deaf and is known for his sense of humor and friendly demeanor. He enjoys making others laugh and often uses humor to connect with his peers. How might a teacher capitalize on James' disposition to establish rapport and support his social integration?

    A. Encouraging James to participate in class discussions using humor to engage his peers.
    B. Discouraging James from using humor, as it may disrupt the classroom environment.
    C. Avoiding interactions with James to prevent disruptions caused by his sense of humor.
    D. Placing James in a self-contained classroom for students with hearing impairments.

Answer:

QUESTION 108

Maria is a 14-year-old student who is deaf and uses cochlear implants. She has a strong interest in science and enjoys conducting experiments. Maria's teacher is looking for specialized materials to support her in conducting hands-on science experiments. Where would Maria's teacher be most likely to find specialized materials tailored for students who are deaf or hard of hearing to facilitate hands-on science experiments?

    A.   Contacting organizations that specialize in producing educational materials for students with hearing impairments.
    B.   Visiting the local library to search for materials related to science experiments for students with hearing impairments.
    C.   Consulting with the school's general education science teacher for recommendations on specialized materials.
    D.   Contacting a local art supply store to inquire about materials for hands-on science experiments.

Answer:

QUESTION 109

Alex is a 10-year-old student who is hard of hearing. He is interested in history and enjoys reading about ancient civilizations. Alex's teacher is looking for specialized materials that provide historical information in a format accessible to students with hearing impairments. Where might Alex's teacher find specialized materials that offer historical content in a format accessible to students with hearing impairments?

    A.   Exploring online resources provided by organizations dedicated to creating accessible educational materials.
    B.   Consulting with a local sports equipment store for materials related to ancient civilizations.
    C.   Visiting a local theater for historical reenactments to engage Alex in hands-on learning.
    D.   Contacting the school's physical education teacher for recommendations on historical content.

Answer:

QUESTION 110

Sophia is a 12-year-old student who is deaf and has a passion for art. She enjoys creating visual artworks using various mediums. Sophia's teacher is searching for specialized art supplies that are suitable for students with hearing impairments. Where might Sophia's teacher find specialized art supplies that are designed to accommodate the needs of students who are deaf or hard of hearing?

    A.   Contacting art supply stores that carry products specifically designed for students with sensory disabilities.
    B.   Visiting a local electronics store to inquire about art supplies suitable for students with hearing impairments.
    C.   Consulting with the school's physical education teacher for recommendations on art supplies.
    D.   Contacting a local music store to inquire about specialized art supplies.

Answer:

QUESTION 111

James is a 16-year-old student who is hard of hearing and has a keen interest in technology. He enjoys using assistive technology devices to support his learning. James's teacher is looking for specialized technology resources to further enhance his educational experience. Where might James's teacher find specialized technology resources and devices tailored for students who are hard of hearing?

    A.   Contacting organizations or agencies specializing in assistive technology for individuals with hearing impairments.
    B.   Visiting a local sports equipment store to inquire about technological devices.
    C.   Consulting with the school's general education technology teacher for recommendations on specialized resources.
    D.   Contacting a local music store to inquire about technology resources for students who are hard of hearing.

Answer:

QUESTION 112

Michael is a 13-year-old student who is deaf and primarily communicates through spoken English. His recent communication assessment data indicates proficiency in lip reading and spoken language. However, he struggles with complex written language. Based on Michael's assessment data, what instructional method might be most effective in addressing his educational needs?

    A. Implementing a multisensory approach that combines visual cues with spoken language to reinforce comprehension.
    B. Focusing solely on written language instruction to improve Michael's proficiency in this area.
    C. Exclusively utilizing spoken language instruction without incorporating visual cues or supports.
    D. Recommending sign language instruction as the primary mode of communication for Michael.

Answer:

QUESTION 113

Emma is an 11-year-old student who is hard of hearing. She communicates primarily through sign language. Emma's communication assessment data indicates strong proficiency in expressive sign language skills, but she faces challenges in written language. Considering Emma's assessment data, what evidence-based communication practice might be most effective in instructing her?

    A. Incorporating visual supports and graphic organizers to facilitate written language comprehension.
    B. Providing exclusive instruction in written language to address Emma's challenges in this area.
    C. Focusing solely on expressive sign language without incorporating written language instruction.
    D. Recommending additional speech therapy sessions to improve Emma's written language skills.

Answer:

QUESTION 114

Sophie is a 14-year-old student who is deaf and primarily communicates through a combination of sign language and written English. Her recent communication assessment data indicates proficiency in both modalities, but she struggles with complex auditory input. Based on Sophie's assessment data, what instructional method might be most effective in addressing her educational needs?

    A. Providing visual and written supports for auditory content to enhance comprehension.
    B. Focusing exclusively on auditory instruction to strengthen Sophie's auditory processing skills.
    C. Relying solely on sign language instruction without incorporating written supports.
    D. Recommending additional speech therapy sessions to improve Sophie's auditory processing.

Answer:

QUESTION 115

Liam is a 15-year-old student who is hard of hearing and primarily communicates through spoken language. His recent communication assessment data indicates challenges in articulation and phonological skills. Based on Liam's assessment data, what evidence-based communication practice might be most effective in instructing him?

    A. Implementing speech therapy sessions that focus on articulation and phonological skills.
    B. Exclusively utilizing sign language instruction to circumvent Liam's challenges in spoken language.
    C. Providing additional written language instruction to compensate for Liam's articulation difficulties.
    D. Ignoring Liam's articulation challenges to focus on other academic areas.

Answer:

QUESTION 116

Nina is a 12-year-old student who is deaf and primarily communicates through a combination of sign language and written English. Her recent communication assessment data indicates proficiency in both modalities. However, she requires additional support in complex auditory comprehension. Considering Nina's assessment data, what instructional method might be most effective in addressing her educational needs?

    A. Providing visual and written supports for complex auditory content to enhance comprehension.
    B. Focusing exclusively on auditory instruction to strengthen Nina's auditory processing skills.
    C. Relying solely on sign language instruction without incorporating written supports.
    D. Recommending additional speech therapy sessions to improve Nina's auditory processing.

Answer:

QUESTION 117

Evan is a 16-year-old student who is hard of hearing and primarily communicates through spoken language. His recent communication assessment data indicates proficiency in articulation and phonological skills. However, he faces challenges in understanding complex written material. Based on Evan's assessment data, what evidence-based communication practice might be most effective in instructing him?

    A. Implementing a structured approach to reading instruction that targets Evan's specific challenges in understanding complex written material.
    B. Exclusively utilizing sign language instruction to circumvent Evan's challenges in understanding written language.
    C. Providing additional speech therapy sessions to further develop Evan's articulation and phonological skills.
    D. Ignoring Evan's challenges in understanding written material and focusing solely on spoken language instruction.

Answer:

QUESTION 118

Emily is a 9-year-old student who is deaf and communicates primarily through American Sign Language (ASL). She has recently transitioned to a mainstream classroom with appropriate supports. Emily is struggling to navigate social interactions with her hearing peers. What strategy might be most effective in teaching Emily appropriate social skills for successful integration into her mainstream classroom?

    A. Facilitating structured peer interactions that incorporate ASL and promote effective communication between Emily and her classmates.
    B. Encouraging Emily to rely solely on written communication to foster independence in social interactions.
    C. Suggesting that Emily communicate exclusively with other students who are deaf or hard of hearing.
    D. Advocating for Emily's return to a self-contained classroom for students with hearing impairments.

Answer:

QUESTION 119

Joshua is a 14-year-old student who is hard of hearing and is known for his strong self-advocacy skills. He is actively involved in his Individualized Education Program (IEP) meetings and expresses his preferences and needs clearly. What strategy might be most effective in further enhancing Joshua's self-awareness and self-advocacy skills?

    A. Encouraging Joshua to reflect on his learning preferences, strengths, and areas of need, and incorporate this self-awareness into his IEP meetings.
    B. Minimizing Joshua's involvement in his IEP meetings to avoid overwhelming him with decisions.
    C. Assigning a teacher to make all decisions regarding Joshua's educational plan to streamline the process.
    D. Excluding Joshua from his IEP meetings to allow the professionals to make decisions on his behalf.

Answer:

QUESTION 120

Lila is a 12-year-old student who is deaf and communicates primarily through spoken language and speechreading. She has recently expressed interest in joining the school's drama club, which involves participating in various social activities. What strategy might be most effective in teaching Lila appropriate social skills for her involvement in the drama club?

- A. Providing Lila with opportunities for role-playing and practicing social interactions in a supportive environment.
- B. Discouraging Lila from joining the drama club to avoid potential social challenges.
- C. Suggesting that Lila communicate solely through written notes to ensure clear communication.
- D. Excluding Lila from social activities to prevent potential difficulties.

Answer:

QUESTION 121

Miguel is a 16-year-old student who is hard of hearing and is transitioning to post-secondary education. He is eager to explore his career options and is considering enrolling in a vocational training program. What strategy might be most effective in enhancing Miguel's self-awareness and independence as he prepares for post-secondary education and vocational training?

- A. Encouraging Miguel to explore various career options, interests, and skills through internships and vocational assessments.
- B. Making all post-secondary education and career decisions on Miguel's behalf to ensure a smooth transition.
- C. Discouraging Miguel from pursuing vocational training and focusing solely on traditional academic paths.
- D. Excluding Miguel from career exploration activities to simplify the transition process.

Answer:

QUESTION 122

Olivia is a 13-year-old student who is deaf and communicates primarily through written English. She is known for her assertiveness and strong sense of responsibility. What strategy might be most effective in further enhancing Olivia's assertiveness and sense of responsibility?

- A. Providing opportunities for Olivia to take on leadership roles and make decisions in collaborative projects.
- B. Discouraging Olivia from taking on any additional responsibilities to avoid potential overwhelm.
- C. Assigning all responsibilities to Olivia without considering her preferences or strengths.
- D. Excluding Olivia from collaborative projects to minimize potential challenges.

Answer:

QUESTION 123

Isaac is a 15-year-old student who is hard of hearing and is known for his independence. He is interested in learning practical life skills, such as cooking and budgeting. What strategy might be most effective in further enhancing Isaac's independence and practical life skills?

- A. Encouraging Isaac to actively participate in cooking and budgeting activities, providing guidance and support as needed.
- B. Taking over all cooking and budgeting activities for Isaac to ensure they are completed accurately.
- C. Discouraging Isaac from participating in practical life skills activities to avoid potential challenges.
- D. Excluding Isaac from practical life skills activities to simplify his daily routine.

Answer:

QUESTION 124

Jamie is a 10-year-old student who is deaf and comes from a culturally and linguistically diverse background. Their family primarily communicates using American Sign Language (ASL), while English is the language of instruction at school. The family places a strong emphasis on maintaining their cultural and linguistic heritage. What is a critical consideration for Jamie's teacher to foster a strong home-school connection in this situation?

A. Actively involving Jamie's family in the development of their Individualized Education Program (IEP) to ensure their cultural and linguistic preferences are reflected.
B. Encouraging Jamie's family to exclusively use English at home to align with the language of instruction at school.
C. Suggesting that Jamie's family solely rely on written communication to bridge the gap between home and school.
D. Minimizing the involvement of Jamie's family in the educational process to avoid potential conflicts.

Answer:

QUESTION 125

Mila is a 14-year-old student who is deaf and comes from a family with limited English proficiency. Her parents primarily communicate in their native language, which is not English. They express concerns about their ability to support Mila's education due to language barriers. What might be an effective strategy for Mila's teacher to address the potential impact of language differences on Mila's educational progress?

A. Implementing strategies to provide information and communicate with Mila's parents in their native language, ensuring they are informed and involved in her education.
B. Discouraging Mila's parents from using their native language at home to encourage English proficiency.
C. Suggesting that Mila's parents rely solely on written communication in English to bridge the language gap.
D. Minimizing communication with Mila's parents to avoid potential language barriers.

Answer:

QUESTION 126

Ethan is a 12-year-old student who is deaf and has recently experienced a significant change in family dynamics due to his parents' divorce. This change has raised concerns about its potential impact on Ethan's well-being and academic performance. What might be a critical step for Ethan's teacher in supporting him through this transition in his family system?

A. Establishing open and regular communication with both of Ethan's parents to gather insights and address any concerns related to his well-being and academic progress.
B. Suggesting that Ethan's parents exclusively communicate through written messages to maintain a clear record of discussions.
C. Minimizing communication with Ethan's parents to avoid potential conflicts arising from the divorce.
D. Encouraging Ethan's parents to make all decisions regarding his education without the teacher's input.

Answer:

QUESTION 127

Aiden is a 15-year-old student who is deaf and comes from a family that holds strong cultural values related to education. His parents have expressed a desire to be actively involved in his educational journey. What might be an effective strategy for Aiden's teacher to leverage the family's value for education in supporting his academic progress?

A. Encouraging Aiden's parents to actively participate in school activities and collaborate with the teacher to reinforce learning at home.
B. Discouraging Aiden's parents from being involved in his education to allow him more independence.
C. Suggesting that Aiden's parents solely rely on written communication to convey their educational expectations.
D. Minimizing Aiden's parents' involvement in school activities to prevent potential conflicts.

Answer:

QUESTION 128

Sophie is a 13-year-old student who is deaf and comes from a family with diverse cultural values. Her parents have expressed concerns about potential conflicts between their values and those emphasized at school. What might be a critical consideration for Sophie's teacher in addressing potential conflicts between the family's values and those emphasized at school?

A. Engaging in open and respectful dialogue with Sophie's parents to gain a deeper understanding of their cultural values and finding ways to integrate them into the educational experience.
B. Insisting that the family strictly adhere to the values emphasized at school to ensure consistency in Sophie's education.
C. Minimizing communication with Sophie's parents to avoid potential conflicts arising from differing values.
D. Encouraging Sophie's parents to conform entirely to the values emphasized at school without any room for negotiation.

Answer:

QUESTION 129

A school district is considering adopting a new approach to the education of children who are deaf or hard of hearing. One proposal emphasizes a person-centered planning approach, focusing on individual needs and goals. Another proposal advocates for a standardized curriculum to ensure consistency across classrooms. What is a critical consideration for the stakeholders in this decision-making process?

A. Evaluating how each approach aligns with the unique needs and goals of individual students who are deaf or hard of hearing.
B. Adopting the standardized curriculum approach to maintain consistency, regardless of individual student needs.
C. Prioritizing cultural perspectives over medical perspectives to guide the decision-making process.
D. Implementing both approaches simultaneously to address a wider range of student needs.

Answer:

QUESTION 130

Aiden is a 12-year-old student who is deaf. His parents have expressed concerns about his educational progress and believe he may benefit from additional support services. They are unsure about their rights and responsibilities in this matter. What is a critical responsibility of Aiden's parents in advocating for his educational needs?

A. Seeking clarification on their rights under the Individuals with Disabilities Education Act (IDEA) and actively participating in the Individualized Education Program (IEP) process.
B. Allowing the school to make all decisions regarding Aiden's education to avoid potential conflicts.
C. Requesting that Aiden be placed in a self-contained classroom for students who are deaf or hard of hearing.
D. Refraining from participating in the IEP process to allow the school to make unbiased decisions.

Answer:

QUESTION 131

Sophia is a 16-year-old student who is hard of hearing. Her parents are concerned about the adequacy of the services provided at her current school and are considering requesting a different placement. What is an important legal standard that Sophia's parents should be aware of when considering a change in her educational placement?

A. The right to a Free Appropriate Public Education (FAPE), which ensures that Sophia receives an education tailored to her needs at no cost to her parents.
B. The exclusive authority of the school in determining the most appropriate educational placement for Sophia, regardless of parental input.
C. The obligation of Sophia's parents to cover any additional costs associated with a change in her educational placement.
D. The school's right to deny any request for a change in placement, even if it is in Sophia's best interest.

Answer:

QUESTION 132

The Smith family recently moved to a new state. Their child, Liam, who is deaf, is transitioning to a new school. The parents are concerned about the eligibility process for special education services in their new school district. What is a key right that the Smith family should be aware of during the eligibility process for special education services in their new school district?

    A.   The right to participate in and consent to the evaluation process, including providing input on assessment tools and methods used.

    B.   The obligation to accept the eligibility decision made by the school district without any parental input.

    C.   The requirement to cover the costs associated with the evaluation process for Liam.

    D.   The right to bypass the evaluation process and immediately receive special education services.

Answer:

QUESTION 133

Ella, a 14-year-old student who is deaf, is experiencing challenges in her current educational placement. Her parents believe that a different placement might better meet her needs. What is a critical step that Ella's parents should take if they wish to request a change in her educational placement?

    A.   Communicating their concerns to the school and requesting an IEP team meeting to discuss potential alternative placements.

    B.   Making the decision to unilaterally change Ella's placement without involving the school.

    C.   Keeping their concerns to themselves to avoid potential conflicts with the school.

    D.   Requesting a change in placement directly from the school district's administrative office.

Answer:

QUESTION 134

Mateo, a 13-year-old student who is hard of hearing, has experienced difficulties in the referral and assessment process for special education services. His parents are uncertain about their rights in this situation. What is an important right that Mateo's parents should be aware of regarding the referral and assessment process for special education services?

    A.   The right to be actively involved in the referral and assessment process, including providing input and consent for evaluations.

    B.   The obligation to accept the school's decision without any parental input in the referral and assessment process.

    C.   The responsibility to cover the costs associated with the referral and assessment process for Mateo.

    D.   The right to bypass the referral and assessment process and immediately receive special education services.

Answer:

QUESTION 135

Sarah is a 10-year-old student who is deaf and communicates through American Sign Language (ASL). She has an Individualized Education Program (IEP) that outlines specific accommodations and services. Sarah's teacher is responsible for maintaining accurate records related to her educational progress. What is a critical consideration for Sarah's teacher in maintaining records while ensuring confidentiality?

    A.   Storing Sarah's records in a secure location accessible only to authorized personnel and ensuring that any electronic records are password-protected.

    B.   Sharing Sarah's records with colleagues to facilitate collaboration without seeking parental consent.

    C.   Keeping paper copies of Sarah's records in a public area for easy access by anyone interested in her progress.

    D.   Sending electronic copies of Sarah's records to parents without encryption to ensure they receive the information promptly.

Answer:

QUESTION 136

Alex is a 15-year-old student who is hard of hearing. He is highly motivated and actively participates in his educational planning. His parents have requested access to his records to stay informed about his progress. What is an appropriate step for Alex's teacher to take in response to his parents' request for access to his records?

    A. Providing Alex's parents with access to his records while ensuring that any sensitive information about other students is redacted.
    B. Denying Alex's parents access to his records to maintain his privacy.
    C. Sharing Alex's records with other professionals involved in his education without parental consent.
    D. Discouraging Alex from involving his parents in his educational planning to promote independence.

Answer:

QUESTION 137

Emma is a 13-year-old student who is deaf and comes from a family with strong cultural values regarding privacy. Her parents are concerned about the confidentiality of her educational records. What is an important consideration for Emma's teacher in respecting her family's cultural values while maintaining accurate records?

    A. Seeking consent from Emma's parents before sharing any information related to her progress or educational plan.
    B. Automatically sharing Emma's records with all stakeholders to ensure transparency.
    C. Avoiding documentation altogether to respect Emma's family's cultural values.
    D. Keeping all records confidential and not sharing any information with Emma's parents.

Answer:

QUESTION 138

Daniel is a 16-year-old student who is hard of hearing. He is transitioning to post-secondary education and is preparing to advocate for his own accommodations and services. What is a critical consideration for Daniel in advocating for his own access to his educational records?

    A. Familiarizing himself with his rights under the Family Educational Rights and Privacy Act (FERPA) and understanding how to request and review his records.
    B. Assuming that all information regarding his educational progress is automatically accessible to him without any action on his part.
    C. Relying solely on his parents to handle all matters related to his educational records.
    D. Ignoring his rights under FERPA and focusing solely on his academic performance.

Answer:

QUESTION 139

You have a deaf student with a strong preference for auditory learning. However, their reading skills are below grade level. What strategy should you implement to improve their reading skills while respecting their learning style?

    A. Encourage the student to focus exclusively on auditory materials.
    B. Provide additional opportunities for listening to audiobooks.
    C. Assign more written materials to improve their reading skills.
    D. Incorporate visual aids and multimedia alongside written materials.

Answer:

QUESTION 140

You are working with a group of deaf or hard of hearing students who have varying learning styles. What is the primary benefit of recognizing and accommodating these diverse learning styles in your teaching approach?

A. Ensuring uniformity in classroom instruction.
B. Addressing individual needs and maximizing learning potential.
C. Reducing the need for specialized teaching methods.
D. Promoting auditory-based learning for all students.

Answer:

QUESTION 141

You are a special education teacher working with a diverse group of deaf students. Among them, one student exhibits a strong preference for tactile learning. They thrive when they can touch and manipulate objects to understand concepts. Another student is a visual learner, while a third student prefers auditory learning. How can you plan an inclusive lesson that accommodates these diverse learning styles and maximizes learning outcomes for all?

A. Use primarily auditory teaching methods and encourage students to adapt.
B. Assign separate tasks for each learning style, ensuring fairness.
C. Incorporate tactile elements, visual aids, and spoken explanations in the lesson.
D. Focus exclusively on visual materials to appeal to the visual learner.

Answer:

QUESTION 142

You have a hard of hearing student with a strong preference for visual learning in a mainstream classroom. The class is currently working on a science project that requires students to conduct experiments and present their findings. How can you best support this student's learning style and their participation in the project?

A. Assign additional reading materials to complement the project.
B. Encourage the student to observe and document the experiments visually.
C. Request a sign language interpreter for all science classes.
D. Suggest the student participate in a different project unrelated to science.

Answer:

QUESTION 143

You have a deaf student who excels in spatial learning and problem-solving. However, the current curriculum primarily emphasizes written assignments and reading comprehension. The student's performance in these areas is below grade level. How can you address this situation to support their spatial learning style while improving their academic performance?

A. Assign more reading assignments to improve their reading skills.
B. Encourage the student to focus on improving their written expression.
C. Provide hands-on activities and projects related to the curriculum.
D. Suggest that the student switch to a school with a different curriculum.

Answer:

QUESTION 144

You are a special education teacher working with a deaf student who uses American Sign Language (ASL) as their primary mode of communication. The standardized assessment for reading comprehension is primarily written. How can you modify this assessment to make it more accessible for the student?

A. Provide the assessment in written form with no modifications.
B. Allow the student to respond to the assessment s in ASL.
C. Use only multiple-choice s to simplify the assessment.
D. Assign a sign language interpreter to translate the assessment.

Answer:

QUESTION 145

You have a diverse group of deaf students in your classroom, some of whom are from culturally and linguistically diverse backgrounds. You are tasked with conducting an assessment to measure their mathematical problem-solving skills. How can you ensure that the assessment is nonbiased and culturally sensitive?

A. Translate the assessment into the students' native languages.
B. Use a variety of assessment formats, including visual and tactile elements.
C. Administer the assessment in a silent environment to eliminate distractions.
D. Provide the same assessment to all students, regardless of their backgrounds.

Answer:

QUESTION 146

You are designing an assessment for a group of hard of hearing students with varying degrees of hearing loss. To ensure the assessment is fair and accessible, what should you consider?

A. Include only multiple-choice s to eliminate subjectivity.
B. Provide written instructions and expect verbal responses.
C. Adjust the assessment's time limits based on the severity of hearing loss.
D. Incorporate visual and written elements into the assessment.

Answer:

QUESTION 147

You have a culturally diverse group of deaf students, each with unique linguistic backgrounds. When selecting assessments, what should be your primary consideration to ensure cultural and linguistic sensitivity?

A. Use assessments developed for the mainstream student population.
B. Focus on assessments that align with the students' cultural backgrounds.
C. Ensure that assessments are administered in the students' native languages.
D. Avoid assessments that require written responses to prevent bias.

Answer:

QUESTION 148

You are conducting a speech and language assessment for a deaf student who primarily communicates using American Sign Language (ASL). The assessment is designed for spoken language. What is the most appropriate modification to make this assessment accessible for the student?

A. Administer the assessment in ASL.
B. Provide the assessment in written form only.
C. Assign a sign language interpreter for the assessment.
D. Use a speech-to-text app for assessment responses.

Answer:

QUESTION 149

You are tasked with assessing the writing skills of a group of deaf students who use sign language as their primary mode of communication. What is the most effective approach to ensure nonbiased assessment of their writing abilities?

    A.   Assign written prompts without considering their sign language proficiency.
    B.   Use a speech recognition software for assessing their writing.
    C.   Develop sign language-based writing prompts for the assessment.
    D.   Allow students to choose whether to respond in written English or sign language.

Answer:

QUESTION 150

You are assessing the reading skills of a deaf student in a classroom setting. The student primarily uses American Sign Language (ASL) for communication. Which assessment method would be most appropriate to evaluate the student's reading comprehension?

    A.   A standardized written test.
    B.   An ASL storytelling assessment.
    C.   An oral reading fluency assessment.
    D.   A multiple-choice naire.

Answer:

QUESTION 151

You are evaluating the writing skills of a hard of hearing student who uses hearing aids and primarily communicates using spoken language. The student has an additional learning disability that affects their writing abilities. What is the most appropriate assessment accommodation to support this student's assessment?

    A.   Providing a sign language interpreter during the assessment.
    B.   Offering extended time to complete the writing assessment.
    C.   Conducting the assessment in a completely silent environment.
    D.   Assigning a scribe to write down the student's responses.

Answer:

QUESTION 152

You are assessing the reading fluency of a group of deaf students who communicate primarily using sign language. What assessment approach is most effective for evaluating their reading fluency?

    A.   Administering a timed oral reading assessment.
    B.   Conducting a sign language storytelling assessment.
    C.   Using a multiple-choice comprehension test.
    D.   Assigning a written reading comprehension assignment.

Answer:

QUESTION 153

You are assessing the writing skills of a group of deaf and hard of hearing students in a diverse classroom. Some students primarily use American Sign Language (ASL), while others use written English. How can you ensure a fair and unbiased writing assessment for all students?

    A.   Administer the assessment only in written English.
    B.   Offer a choice between ASL and written English for responses.
    C.   Assign a sign language interpreter for all students.
    D.   Provide extra time for students who use ASL.

Answer:

QUESTION 154

You are assessing the reading comprehension of a deaf student who uses cochlear implants for communication. The student struggles with spoken language. What is the most suitable assessment accommodation for this student?

    A. Providing the assessment in written form only.
    B. Using a sign language interpreter during the assessment.
    C. Administering the assessment in a quiet, noise-free environment.
    D. Assigning a speech therapist to assist with the assessment.

Answer:

QUESTION 155

You are assessing the writing skills of a deaf student who communicates primarily using spoken language and has a cochlear implant. The student has strong speaking skills but struggles with writing. What assessment modification would be most appropriate for this student?

    A. Offering extra time to complete the writing assessment.
    B. Providing a speech-to-text software for the writing assessment.
    C. Administering the assessment in a noisy environment to mimic real-life distractions.
    D. Assigning a sign language interpreter for the assessment.

Answer:

QUESTION 156

You have a diverse group of deaf and hard of hearing students in your classroom. One student has a cochlear implant, while another primarily uses American Sign Language (ASL) for communication. What is the most effective strategy to create an inclusive learning environment that meets the needs of both students?

    A. Implementing a solely auditory-based teaching approach.
    B. Providing written materials with no modifications.
    C. Incorporating visual aids and gestures alongside spoken language.
    D. Assigning a sign language interpreter for all classes.

Answer

QUESTION 157

You are designing a classroom environment to accommodate the needs of a hard of hearing student who uses hearing aids. What environmental modification should you prioritize to support their learning?

    A. Reducing all classroom noise to an absolute minimum.
    B. Installing soundproof barriers around the student's desk.
    C. Using only written communication to eliminate auditory distractions.
    D. Arranging seating to ensure the student is positioned for optimal sound reception.

Answer:

QUESTION 158

You have a deaf student with additional disabilities in your classroom. To promote their active participation and independence, what strategy should you prioritize?

    A. Reducing their workload to ease their academic challenges.
    B. Providing a one-on-one aide for constant assistance.
    C. Fostering self-advocacy skills and providing appropriate accommodations.
    D. Isolating the student to minimize disruptions in the classroom.

Answer:

QUESTION 159

You have a hard of hearing student who is struggling academically and often feels isolated in the classroom. What action can you take to promote their active participation and sense of belonging?

    A.   Assigning the student additional homework for extra practice.
    B.   Encouraging the student to sit at the back of the classroom for better focus.
    C.   Implementing peer tutoring and involving classmates in supporting the student.
    D.   Providing headphones to eliminate background noise.

Answer:

QUESTION 160

You have a deaf student with a cochlear implant who often misses important auditory cues during group discussions. What strategy can you employ to ensure their active participation in such situations?

    A.   Discourage group discussions and focus on individual work.
    B.   Provide written transcripts of group discussions afterward.
    C.   Assign the student a sign language interpreter for all discussions.
    D.   Use a microphone and speaker system for clarity during discussions.

Answer:

QUESTION 161

You have a hard of hearing student who is not yet advocating for their own needs in the classroom. What is a proactive strategy to encourage self-advocacy and independence?

    A.   Assigning a full-time aide to anticipate and meet the student's needs.
    B.   Relying solely on written communication to eliminate the need for self-advocacy.
    C.   Providing clear information about available support services and encouraging the student to request them.
    D.   Isolating the student to minimize distractions from their peers.

Answer:

QUESTION 162

In your inclusive classroom, you have a deaf student who uses sign language as their primary mode of communication and a hard of hearing student who uses hearing aids. The classroom is not equipped with assistive listening devices, and group discussions are challenging for both students due to background noise. How can you create an inclusive learning environment for these students during group discussions?

    A.   Assign the deaf student a sign language interpreter and provide hearing aids for the hard of hearing student.
    B.   Isolate the two students in a separate quiet room for discussions.
    C.   Use written communication exclusively for group discussions.
    D.   Implement a microphone and speaker system for clarity during discussions.

Answer:

QUESTION 163

You have a hard of hearing student in your class who struggles to actively participate in classroom discussions. This student uses hearing aids, but they often miss important auditory cues. The class has group discussions regularly. How can you support this student's active participation?

    A.   Encourage the student to sit at the front of the classroom.
    B.   Provide written transcripts of group discussions afterward.
    C.   Assign the student a sign language interpreter for all discussions.
    D.   Use a microphone and speaker system for clarity during discussions.

Answer:

QUESTION 164

You have a diverse group of deaf and hard of hearing students in your class. Some use American Sign Language (ASL) as their primary mode of communication, while others rely on hearing aids or cochlear implants. Additionally, you have students with additional disabilities. How can you design an inclusive learning environment that accommodates these diverse needs?

    A.   Implement an ASL-only teaching approach to ensure consistency.
    B.   Assign individual aides to assist each student's unique needs.
    C.   Incorporate a variety of teaching methods, visual aids, and written materials.
    D.   Group students based on their primary mode of communication.

Answer:

QUESTION 165

In your inclusive classroom, you have a deaf student who uses American Sign Language (ASL) as their primary mode of communication. This student excels in math but struggles with reading comprehension. What is the most effective strategy for differentiating instruction to address this student's needs?

    A.   Assign additional math assignments to enhance their strengths.
    B.   Provide written reading materials with no modifications.
    C.   Offer ASL-based reading materials and comprehension support.
    D.   Isolate the student to provide one-on-one reading instruction.

Answer:

QUESTION 166

You have a diverse group of students who are deaf or hard of hearing, each with unique learning profiles. What is a key strategy for planning and implementing differentiated instruction to meet their individual needs?

    A.   Implementing a standardized curriculum for all students.
    B.   Providing additional homework to challenge all students equally.
    C.   Identifying each student's strengths and weaknesses and tailoring instruction accordingly.
    D.   Assigning the same instructional methods to all students.

Answer:

QUESTION 167

You are teaching a mixed-age group of deaf and hard of hearing students, each with varying levels of language proficiency. What strategy can enhance differentiated instruction in this inclusive classroom?

    A.   Grouping students solely based on age.
    B.   Focusing on a single teaching method for all students.
    C.   Creating flexible learning groups based on language proficiency.
    D.   Assigning extra homework for older students to mentor younger ones.

Answer:

QUESTION 168

You have a hard of hearing student with an additional learning disability who struggles with written language. Traditional methods have not been effective in improving their writing skills. What research-based instructional method may be most beneficial for this student?

    A.   Implementing more intensive phonics instruction.
    B.   Focusing on rote memorization of writing rules.
    C.   Incorporating assistive technology for writing support.
    D.   Assigning additional writing assignments for practice.

Answer:

QUESTION 169

You have a diverse group of students who are deaf or hard of hearing in your classroom, and you want to ensure that your instructional materials are research-based and effective. What is a crucial step in selecting and adapting instructional materials for this population?

A. Relying solely on materials provided by the school district.
B. Consulting with a team of specialists to evaluate materials.
C. Assigning the same materials for all students to ensure consistency.
D. Using materials that are popular among mainstream students.

Answer:

QUESTION 170

You are planning instruction for a deaf student with a cochlear implant who is learning to read. What research-based instructional method can be particularly effective in this situation?

A. Using only written materials without auditory support.
B. Incorporating both visual and auditory elements in reading instruction.
C. Isolating the student from group reading activities.
D. Assigning additional reading assignments to improve skills.

Answer:

QUESTION 171

You are a special education teacher working with a deaf student who primarily uses American Sign Language (ASL) for communication. What is a key aspect of ASL structure and grammar that you should be familiar with to effectively support this student's language development?

A. Relying on English grammar rules when using ASL.
B. Using ASL signs in the same order as English words in sentences.
C. Understanding the importance of facial expressions and non-manual markers in ASL.
D. Encouraging the student to use spoken English alongside ASL for clarity.

Answer:

QUESTION 172

You are working with a group of deaf students who are learning ASL as their primary language. What linguistic aspect of ASL should you prioritize when teaching them?

A. Teaching English grammar alongside ASL to improve their overall language skills.
B. Focusing on the written form of ASL to support literacy development.
C. Emphasizing ASL's distinct syntax and sentence structure.
D. Using spoken English as a bridge language for ASL instruction.

Answer:

QUESTION 173

You have a deaf student who is struggling with English grammar and syntax. They primarily use ASL for communication. What approach should you consider to address this student's language difficulties effectively?

A. Focusing solely on ASL and disregarding English instruction.
B. Using spoken English as the primary mode of communication in the classroom.
C. Providing instruction that explicitly compares and contrasts ASL and English.
D. Assigning additional English grammar worksheets for practice.

Answer:

QUESTION 174

You are teaching a group of deaf students about the differences between ASL and English grammar. What is a fundamental distinction that you should highlight?

    A. ASL uses written English grammar rules.
    B. ASL has a subject-verb-object (SVO) word order.
    C. English sentence structure aligns with ASL structure.
    D. ASL has no distinct grammatical features.

Answer:

QUESTION 175

You are planning a lesson on ASL linguistics for your students. What linguistic aspect of ASL should you emphasize to help them grasp the language's complexity?

    A. The use of spoken English as a substitute for ASL in formal settings.
    B. The similarity of ASL grammar to written English.
    C. The rich use of classifiers in ASL to convey specific meanings.
    D. The avoidance of facial expressions in ASL to maintain clarity.

Answer:

QUESTION 176

You have a diverse group of deaf and hard of hearing students in your classroom, each with varying levels of ASL proficiency. What is a key strategy for creating an inclusive learning environment for these students?

    A. Implementing English-only instruction to ensure consistency.
    B. Providing ASL instruction at an advanced level for all students.
    C. Creating flexible learning groups based on ASL proficiency levels.
    D. Assigning additional ASL assignments for practice.

Answer:

QUESTION 177

You are working with a group of deaf students transitioning into adulthood. What is a key strategy for promoting their vocational competence?

    A. Providing isolated vocational training without considering their individual interests and strengths.
    B. Assigning all students the same vocational career path.
    C. Tailoring vocational training to match students' interests and abilities.
    D. Focusing solely on academic skills for vocational success.

Answer:

QUESTION 178

You have a student who is deaf and has expressed an interest in pursuing a career in the arts. How can you evaluate and select appropriate instructional materials and resources to support their career aspirations effectively?

    A. Steer the student toward vocational training in a different field.
    B. Consult with the student to identify relevant instructional materials and community resources.
    C. Provide standardized academic materials for the student's career goals.
    D. Assign the same instructional materials for all students regardless of their interests.

Answer:

QUESTION 179

You are working with a group of deaf students who are transitioning into independent living. What is a key strategy for promoting their functional living skills?

A. Providing scripted scenarios without allowing for practical decision-making.
B. Assigning the same living arrangements for all students.
C. Offering real-life situations and decision-making opportunities.
D. Focusing solely on academic skills for independent living.

Answer:

QUESTION 180

You are tasked with selecting assistive technologies for a group of deaf students to enhance their communication and vocational skills. What should be a primary consideration when evaluating these technologies?

A. Choosing technologies that are primarily designed for hearing individuals.
B. Selecting technologies that are popular among mainstream students.
C. Identifying technologies that are specific to the unique needs of deaf individuals.
D. Assigning the same assistive technologies for all students.

Answer:

QUESTION 181

You are researching effective model programs for deaf and hard of hearing students. What is a key benefit of these programs for special education teachers?

A. Model programs eliminate the need for individualized instruction.
B. Special education teachers can apply the same strategies in all educational settings.
C. Model programs offer proven strategies and best practices to enhance student outcomes.
D. Special education teachers must create entirely new curricula for each program.

Answer:

QUESTION 182

You are tasked with selecting a model program for early childhood education for a group of deaf and hard of hearing children. What should be a primary consideration when choosing the program?

A. Selecting a program without considering the specific needs of the children.
B. Choosing a program solely based on its popularity.
C. Identifying a program that aligns with the unique needs of the children.
D. Assigning the same program for all children regardless of their needs.

Answer:

QUESTION 183

You have a newly enrolled deaf student, and their parents are concerned about the best communication mode for their child. The parents are unsure whether to use American Sign Language (ASL) or spoken English. What is a key strategy for addressing this concern effectively?

A. Persuading the parents to choose ASL for consistency.
B. Making the final decision without involving the parents.
C. Engaging in open communication with the parents to explore their preferences and provide information.
D. Assigning the communication mode based on school policy.

Answer:

QUESTION 184

You have a hard of hearing student who uses hearing aids, and their parents are concerned about their child's academic progress. The parents believe that the child may be struggling due to their hearing loss. What is an effective strategy for addressing this concern?

A. Assuring the parents that hearing aids alone will resolve the academic issues.
B. Disregarding the parents' concerns and focusing solely on academic interventions.
C. Conducting a comprehensive assessment to identify the student's specific needs and strengths.
D. Assigning the student extra homework to catch up with their peers.

Answer:

QUESTION 185

You have a deaf student in your class, and their parents are concerned about their social and emotional well-being. The student has been experiencing feelings of isolation. What is a key strategy for addressing this concern?

A. Isolating the student from the class to prevent disruptions.
B. Suggesting that the student develop coping strategies independently.
C. Implementing peer support and fostering an inclusive classroom community.
D. Assigning more academic work to keep the student occupied.

Answer:

QUESTION 186

You have a deaf student with parents who primarily communicate using spoken English. The student primarily uses American Sign Language (ASL) and struggles with communication at home. What is an effective strategy for facilitating communication between the student and their parents?

A. Insisting that the parents learn ASL to communicate with the student.
B. Assigning the student extra ASL practice to improve communication.
C. Providing resources and training to the parents to support their understanding and use of ASL.
D. Encouraging the student to rely solely on written communication at home.

Answer

QUESTION 187

You have a hard of hearing student in your class, and their parents are concerned about their involvement in extracurricular activities due to their hearing loss. What is an effective strategy for addressing this concern?

A. Discouraging the student from participating in extracurricular activities.
B. Assigning the student additional academic work to compensate for the lack of extracurricular involvement.
C. Collaborating with the student and parents to identify accommodations and support for extracurricular participation.
D. Encouraging the student to focus solely on academic pursuits.

Answer:

QUESTION 188

You have a newly enrolled deaf student, and their parents are concerned about the student's transition to a new school environment. What is a key strategy for addressing this transition concern effectively?

A. Assigning the student extra assignments to help them catch up.
B. Focusing solely on academic aspects of the transition.
C. Holding a meeting with the parents to discuss their concerns and involve them in the transition plan.
D. Isolating the student from the rest of the class to minimize disruptions.

Answer:

QUESTION 189

You are a special education teacher working with a deaf student who is integrated into a general education classroom. The general education teacher is struggling to accommodate the student's needs effectively. What is a key strategy for coaching the general education teacher?

A. Assigning additional work for the general education teacher to address the student's needs.
B. Providing a list of accommodations without further guidance.
C. Collaborating with the general education teacher to co-plan and co-teach lessons.
D. Isolating the deaf student from the general education classroom to minimize disruptions.

Answer:

QUESTION 190

You are working with a group of general education teachers who have deaf or hard of hearing students in their classrooms. What is a key aspect to emphasize when coaching them in the use of instructional methods and accommodations?

A. Encouraging one-size-fits-all teaching methods.
B. Focusing solely on the academic needs of the students.
C. Promoting differentiated instruction and individualized accommodations.
D. Assigning the same accommodations for all deaf and hard of hearing students.

Answer:

QUESTION 191

You have a deaf student with complex communication needs who requires specific assistive technology in the general education classroom. The general education teacher is unfamiliar with these technologies. What is a key strategy for coaching the teacher in using these technologies effectively?

A. Isolating the student to provide one-on-one technology instruction.
B. Assigning the student to a specialized program outside the general education classroom.
C. Collaborating with the teacher and providing training on the assistive technologies.
D. Focusing solely on traditional teaching methods to avoid technology complications.

Answer:

QUESTION 192

You are a special education teacher working with a group of deaf and hard of hearing students. What should be a key consideration when coaching general education teachers in the use of accommodations and technologies?

A. Using accommodations and technologies exclusively for students with hearing loss.
B. Focusing on accommodation implementation without considering the students' individual needs.
C. Ensuring that accommodations and technologies are seamlessly integrated into the general education classroom.
D. Assigning the same accommodations and technologies for all students.

Answer:

QUESTION 193

You are tasked with coaching a general education teacher on accommodating a deaf student who uses American Sign Language (ASL) as their primary mode of communication. What is a key strategy to emphasize in this coaching process?

A. Encouraging the general education teacher to rely solely on spoken language.
B. Focusing solely on academic accommodations without considering communication needs.
C. Promoting the use of visual aids and ASL interpreters to support communication.
D. Isolating the deaf student from the general education classroom to minimize distractions.

Answer:

QUESTION 194

You are working with a group of special education teachers who need to access community agency services for deaf and hard of hearing students. What should be a key consideration when coaching them in accessing and working effectively with such agencies?

    A.   Relying solely on community agency services without any collaboration.
    B.   Overlooking the specific needs of each student when accessing services.
    C.   Building collaborative partnerships and ensuring alignment with students' individual needs.
    D.   Assigning the same community agency services for all students.

Answer:

QUESTION 195

You are a special education teacher working with deaf and hard of hearing students. What is a key strategy for engaging in reflection and self-assessment to improve your instruction and professional growth?

    A.   Avoiding self-assessment to prevent self-doubt.
    B.   Reflecting solely on personal successes without considering challenges.
    C.   Regularly evaluating your teaching practices and seeking feedback from colleagues and students.
    D.   Isolating yourself from professional development opportunities.

Answer:

QUESTION 196

You are a special education teacher working with deaf and hard of hearing students from diverse backgrounds. What is a crucial aspect to consider when engaging in reflection and self-assessment to identify cultural biases?

    A.   Ignoring cultural differences to maintain neutrality.
    B.   Acknowledging and examining your own cultural biases.
    C.   Avoiding interactions with students from diverse backgrounds.
    D.   Isolating yourself from professional development opportunities.

Answer:

QUESTION 197

You are a special education teacher working with deaf students from various cultural backgrounds. During a recent lesson, you noticed that you unintentionally favored students from one particular cultural group. What is the most effective immediate action to take?

    A.   Ignore the situation and continue with the lesson.
    B.   Reflect on the situation, acknowledge the bias, and adjust your teaching approach.
    C.   Apply the same teaching method to all students to avoid favoritism.
    D.   Isolate students from the cultural group to prevent future bias.

Answer:

QUESTION 198

You are a special education teacher aiming to improve your instruction for deaf and hard of hearing students. What is an essential strategy for engaging in reflection and self-assessment to guide your professional growth?

    A.   Avoiding self-assessment to maintain a comfortable teaching routine.
    B.   Seeking feedback only from peers with similar teaching styles.
    C.   Setting clear goals for professional growth and regularly evaluating progress.
    D.   Isolating yourself from professional development opportunities.

Answer:

QUESTION 199

You are a special education teacher focused on improving your communication skills with deaf and hard of hearing students. What is the importance of interacting with deaf adults on a regular basis for communication skills development?

A. Interacting with deaf adults is unnecessary for communication skills development.
B. Deaf adults can provide valuable insights into deaf culture and language.
C. Communication skills can only be developed through classroom instruction.
D. Isolating yourself from interactions with deaf adults promotes better communication.

Answer:

QUESTION 200

You are a special education teacher working with a newly enrolled deaf student. The student's communication skills are limited, and you want to improve your ability to communicate effectively. What is a key strategy to enhance your communication skills in this scenario?

A. Isolating the student from interactions with deaf adults to prevent confusion.
B. Seeking guidance and mentorship from experienced deaf adults or educators.
C. Relying solely on written communication to ensure clarity.
D. Avoiding interactions with the student to prevent potential miscommunication.

Answer:

QUESTION 201

A 5-year-old deaf student exhibits difficulty in forming complex sentences and struggles with vocabulary. However, they excel in problem-solving tasks and spatial reasoning. Which of the following options best explains this observation?

A. The student may have a language processing disorder.
B. The student is likely not receiving appropriate social support.
C. The student's deafness is causing cognitive impairment.
D. The student is gifted in non-verbal cognitive abilities.

Answer:

QUESTION 202

A deaf student and a hearing student both have an Individualized Education Plan (IEP) in a mainstream classroom. What is a key similarity in the IEPs for these two students?

A. The IEPs will both focus on improving hearing abilities.
B. The IEPs will both address their unique educational needs.
C. The IEPs will have identical goals for both students.
D. The IEPs will not be required for either student.

Answer:

QUESTION 203

A family of a deaf child has decided to learn American Sign Language (ASL) alongside their child. How might this impact the child's development?

A. It may hinder the child's communication skills.
B. It can foster a strong bond between the child and their family.
C. It will have no impact on the child's development.
D. It will delay the child's language development.

Answer:

QUESTION 204

A deaf adolescent who excelled academically during elementary school begins to struggle in high school. What is a likely explanation for this change in academic performance?

A. The adolescent is losing their hearing abilities.
B. The transition to high school is inherently challenging for all students.
C. Adolescence often brings social and emotional changes that can impact academics.
D. The adolescent has a learning disability.

Answer:

QUESTION 205

A family of a deaf child is hesitant to use sign language and insists on lip-reading as the primary mode of communication. What potential challenges might this pose for the child's development?

A. It may limit the child's access to language.
B. It will enhance the child's lip-reading skills.
C. It will accelerate the child's language development.
D. It will improve the child's hearing abilities.

Answer:

QUESTION 206

A teacher notices that a deaf student is experiencing social isolation in a mainstream classroom. What is a key consideration when addressing this situation?

A. Deaf students should be separated from their hearing peers to avoid isolation.
B. Social isolation is common for all deaf students and is not a cause for concern.
C. Implementing inclusive practices and fostering peer support can help reduce social isolation.
D. The student's isolation is not the teacher's responsibility.

Answer:

QUESTION 207

Sarah, a deaf student, is struggling academically and socially in school. Her parents, who are also deaf, have chosen to communicate solely through American Sign Language (ASL) at home. They believe this approach will strengthen Sarah's identity within the deaf community. Sarah's teachers are concerned about her language development and social isolation. What should the school consider when addressing this situation?

A. Encourage Sarah's parents to stop using ASL at home.
B. Create a supportive environment that values Sarah's deaf identity while addressing her academic and social needs.
C. Recommend that Sarah transfer to a school for deaf students exclusively.
D. Require Sarah to communicate only in spoken language at school.

Answer:

QUESTION 208

Mark, a hard of hearing student, excels in mathematics but struggles with reading and writing. His teachers have noticed that he often appears frustrated and unmotivated in language-based tasks. Mark's parents are concerned about his academic progress. What is a potential explanation for Mark's academic strengths and weaknesses, and how should the school address it?

A. Mark may have a learning disability, and the school should conduct a formal assessment.
B. Mark's hearing loss is causing cognitive impairment, and he should be placed in special education classes.
C. Mark's strengths and weaknesses may be influenced by his individual learning style, and the school should provide targeted support.
D. Mark's academic performance is solely a result of his effort, and no additional support is needed.

Answer:

QUESTION 209

Alex, a deaf student, is part of a mainstream classroom where he is the only student with a hearing impairment. He often faces communication challenges with his hearing peers, which result in social isolation. The teacher is committed to fostering an inclusive environment. What steps should the teacher take to promote social inclusion for Alex?

    A.   Isolate Alex from the hearing students to avoid communication difficulties.

    B.   Organize separate social activities exclusively for deaf students.

    C.   Implement inclusive practices, such as peer support and communication strategies, to facilitate interaction between Alex and his hearing peers.

    D.   Place the responsibility for inclusion solely on Alex and his hearing peers.

Answer:

QUESTION 210

A 5-year-old deaf child who uses American Sign Language (ASL) shows significant improvement in their expressive signing skills but struggles with understanding complex ASL sentences. What might this observation suggest?

    A.   The child is not motivated to learn ASL.

    B.   The child has a cognitive impairment.

    C.   The child's receptive ASL skills are developing more slowly.

    D.   The child's hearing abilities are improving.

Answer:

QUESTION 211

A teacher is working with a newly identified deaf student who has profound hearing loss. The child's parents have decided against using hearing aids or cochlear implants. What should the teacher consider when planning educational support for this student?

    A.   The child will not benefit from any educational interventions.

    B.   The teacher should focus solely on visual teaching methods.

    C.   The teacher should explore alternative communication options like sign language.

    D.   The teacher should persuade the parents to reconsider hearing aids or implants.

Answer:

QUESTION 212

A 12-year-old deaf student who primarily uses Sign Supported English (SSE) in the classroom is struggling with English language literacy skills. What might be a potential challenge for this student?

    A.   SSE is a highly effective method for English language literacy.

    B.   The student may not have been exposed to sufficient English text.

    C.   The student's hearing loss is improving.

    D.   The student has a natural talent for learning English.

Answer:

QUESTION 213

Two children, one born with hearing loss and one who acquired hearing loss later in life, are enrolled in the same classroom. What might be a significant factor impacting their learning experiences?

    A.   The children's hearing loss is the only relevant factor.

    B.   The age at which the hearing loss occurred.

    C.   The children's intelligence levels.

    D.   The presence of hearing aids or cochlear implants.

Answer:

QUESTION 214

A teacher notices that a 7-year-old deaf student, who primarily uses American Sign Language (ASL), is becoming increasingly proficient in ASL storytelling but struggles with reading comprehension in English. What is a possible explanation for this discrepancy?

- A. The student is not interested in learning to read in English.
- B. The student's English reading skills are age-appropriate.
- C. The student's ASL storytelling skills are influencing their English reading development.
- D. The student's hearing abilities have improved.

Answer:

QUESTION 215

A teacher is working with a deaf student whose parents are actively involved in the deaf community and have strong cultural and linguistic ties. What should the teacher consider when planning this student's education?

- A. The teacher should focus exclusively on speech and auditory development.
- B. The student's cultural and linguistic background should be respected and integrated into their education.
- C. The teacher should encourage the student to isolate themselves from the deaf community.
- D. The student's parents should be discouraged from participating in the education process.

Answer:

QUESTION 216

A preschool-aged deaf child is exposed to American Sign Language (ASL) from birth and receives regular language-rich interactions with their family and educators. What is the potential benefit of this early and meaningful exposure to ASL?

- A. The child will have delayed language development due to the use of ASL.
- B. The child is more likely to develop age-appropriate linguistic and cognitive skills.
- C. ASL exposure will have no impact on the child's development.
- D. The child will rely solely on lip-reading for communication.

Answer:

QUESTION 217

A middle school teacher is working with a hard of hearing student who was exposed to spoken language from an early age but did not receive early intervention services. The student struggles with reading comprehension. What might be a potential factor contributing to this difficulty?

- A. Early exposure to spoken language is sufficient for reading comprehension development.
- B. Lack of early intervention services may have delayed language development.
- C. The student's hearing loss has improved over time.
- D. The student is not motivated to read.

Answer:

QUESTION 218

A high school teacher is working with a deaf student who primarily uses sign language and has strong linguistic skills in American Sign Language (ASL). However, the student struggles with written English composition. What might explain this discrepancy?

- A. The student is not interested in learning written English.
- B. Strong ASL skills do not correlate with written English skills.
- C. The student's hearing abilities have improved.
- D. The student's ASL skills are impeding their English composition.

Answer:

QUESTION 219

A teacher is working with a deaf student who was not exposed to any formal language until the age of 7 due to a lack of early intervention services. The student is now struggling with language and communication skills. What should the teacher consider when planning support for this student?

A. The student will never develop language skills.
B. Intensive speech therapy is the only effective intervention.
C. Providing language-rich environments and alternative communication methods is crucial.
D. The student's struggles are a result of laziness.

Answer:

QUESTION 220

A preschool-aged hard of hearing child has received early intervention services that focus on spoken language development. The child's family is committed to creating a language-rich environment at home. What is a potential benefit of this approach?

A. The child will not develop age-appropriate language skills.
B. The child is more likely to develop age-appropriate linguistic and cognitive skills.
C. Early intervention services are not effective for hard of hearing children.
D. The child will solely rely on sign language for communication.

Answer:

QUESTION 221

Emily, a deaf child, was diagnosed with hearing loss at birth. She received early intervention services that emphasized the development of spoken language skills. However, her progress in language development has been slow, and she struggles with academic tasks. Emily's family is now considering introducing American Sign Language (ASL) into her communication. What should the family consider when making this decision?

A. ASL may further delay Emily's language development.
B. Introducing ASL may help bridge gaps in Emily's language development.
C. ASL will have no impact on Emily's language skills.
D. Emily should continue with speech-only interventions.

Answer:

QUESTION 222

Alex, a hard of hearing teenager, has been using spoken language as his primary mode of communication since childhood. Despite consistent speech therapy and hearing aids, his language skills remain below grade level. Alex's family is considering introducing sign language to support his communication and academic success. What potential benefits might arise from incorporating sign language into Alex's life?

A. Sign language will hinder Alex's speech development.
B. Sign language may provide a supplementary means of communication and improve language skills.
C. Sign language will replace spoken language completely.
D. Sign language is not appropriate for teenagers.

Answer:

QUESTION 223

Sarah, a deaf child, was exposed to American Sign Language (ASL) from infancy and has been part of a signing Deaf community. She excels in her ASL communication skills, but her written English skills are below grade level. Sarah's parents are considering enrolling her in an English-focused language program. What should they consider when making this decision?

A. Sarah's ASL skills may hinder her English language development.
B. Sarah's ASL skills are sufficient for English literacy.
C. Sarah's English skills will naturally catch up with her ASL skills.
D. Sarah should continue with ASL exclusively for communication.

Answer:

QUESTION 224

A teacher is tasked with assessing the auditory skills of a newly identified deaf student. Which assessment method is most suitable for evaluating the child's auditory discrimination and sound identification skills?

A. A standardized written test.
B. An expressive language assessment.
C. An audiogram.
D. An informal listening comprehension task.

Answer:

QUESTION 225

A special education teacher is evaluating the speech skills of a hard of hearing student who has a speech disorder. Which assessment method is most appropriate for assessing the student's articulation and speech production?

A. A hearing screening test.
B. A receptive language assessment.
C. A standardized articulation test.
D. An expressive writing task.

Answer:

QUESTION 226

A teacher is conducting an assessment of a deaf student's receptive language skills. Which assessment tool would be most appropriate for evaluating the student's ability to understand and follow spoken instructions?

A. A vocabulary quiz.
B. A speech production assessment.
C. A standardized receptive language test.
D. An audiogram.

Answer:

QUESTION 227

A teacher is assessing the expressive language skills of a deaf student with an additional intellectual disability. What should the teacher consider when selecting appropriate assessment methods?

A. Use only standardized assessments to ensure objectivity.
B. Consider the student's intellectual disability and choose assessments that are appropriate for their cognitive level.
C. Focus on assessing receptive language skills instead.
D. Rely on teacher observations without formal assessments.

Answer:

QUESTION 228

A teacher is conducting an informal assessment of a deaf student's auditory skills. What might be an appropriate task to include in this assessment?

    A.   Administering a standardized reading comprehension test.
    B.   Observing the student's ability to follow spoken directions.
    C.   Conducting a hearing screening test.
    D.   Evaluating the student's speech production skills.

Answer:

QUESTION 229

A teacher is assessing the speech skills of a deaf student with additional physical disabilities that limit their motor control. Which approach should the teacher consider for this assessment?

    A.   Focus on evaluating the student's sign language skills instead of speech.
    B.   Use only standardized assessments designed for typical speech development.
    C.   Modify assessment methods to accommodate the student's physical limitations.
    D.   Rely on parent reports for speech assessment.

Answer:

QUESTION 230

A special education teacher is reviewing the results of a reading assessment for a deaf student. The assessment indicates that the student struggles with decoding skills but excels in reading comprehension. What is a possible interpretation of these results?

    A.   The student has a learning disability.
    B.   The student's reading challenges are solely related to comprehension.
    C.   The student may have strong compensatory strategies.
    D.   The assessment is unreliable.

Answer:

QUESTION 231

A special education teacher needs to communicate the reading assessment results of a deaf student to the student's parents. What approach should the teacher consider for effective communication?

    A.   Provide a lengthy written report with technical language.
    B.   Share a simplified summary of results with clear explanations.
    C.   Avoid involving parents in the assessment process.
    D.   Rely on the student to explain the results to their parents.

Answer:

QUESTION 232

A teacher is assessing the writing skills of a deaf student and notices that the student consistently struggles with grammatical accuracy but demonstrates creativity and strong storytelling abilities. What might be a potential interpretation of these results?

    A.   The student has a severe writing disability.
    B.   The student's writing challenges are due to a lack of creativity.
    C.   The student may benefit from grammar-focused interventions.
    D.   The assessment is invalid.

Answer:

QUESTION 233

A special education teacher is working with a deaf student who has made significant progress in reading skills. How should the teacher communicate this positive progress to the student?

    A. Avoid mentioning progress to prevent complacency.
    B. Provide detailed technical data on progress.
    C. Celebrate the student's achievements and set new goals.
    D. Communicate progress only to the student's parents.

Answer:

QUESTION 234

A teacher is reviewing the results of a reading assessment for a deaf student and notices that the student struggles with both decoding and reading comprehension. What might be an appropriate interpretation of these results?

    A. The student is not motivated to learn to read.
    B. The student may have a severe reading disability.
    C. The assessment is unreliable.
    D. The student's reading challenges are solely due to a lack of effort.

Answer:

QUESTION 235

A special education teacher has assessed the writing skills of a deaf student and needs to communicate the results to the student's general education teacher. What approach should the teacher consider for effective communication?

    A. Share only the areas of concern and do not highlight any strengths.
    B. Provide a detailed report with technical language.
    C. Collaborate with the general education teacher to discuss the results together.
    D. Keep the results confidential and not share them with the general education teacher.

Answer:

QUESTION 236

Sarah is a deaf high school student who recently completed a reading assessment. The results indicate that she struggles with both decoding and reading comprehension. Her special education teacher, Mr. Johnson, is reviewing the findings. What interpretation and action should Mr. Johnson consider based on these results?

    A. Conclude that Sarah has a severe reading disability and recommend targeted interventions.
    B. Assume that Sarah is not putting in enough effort and encourage her to read more.
    C. Disregard the results as unreliable and repeat the assessment.
    D. Focus solely on Sarah's strengths and avoid addressing her reading challenges.

Answer

QUESTION 237

John, a deaf elementary school student, has shown significant progress in his writing skills, as indicated by recent assessments. His special education teacher, Ms. Martinez, wants to communicate this positive progress to John's parents effectively. What approach should Ms. Martinez consider for sharing the assessment results with John's parents?

    A. Provide a detailed technical report with complex terminology.
    B. Share only the areas where John needs improvement to maintain a balanced perspective.
    C. Arrange a meeting with John's parents to celebrate his achievements and set new goals.
    D. Avoid discussing the assessment results with John's parents to prevent unnecessary stress.

Answer:

52

QUESTION 238

Maria is a deaf student in middle school who recently underwent a comprehensive reading assessment. The results indicate that Maria excels in decoding but struggles with reading comprehension. Her special education teacher, Mr. Anderson, is tasked with sharing these results with Maria's general education teacher. What approach should Mr. Anderson consider for effective communication?

   A.   Share only the areas where Maria excels to maintain a positive perspective.
   B.   Provide a lengthy written report with technical language to ensure precision.
   C.   Collaborate with the general education teacher to discuss the results and develop targeted strategies.
   D.   Keep the results confidential and do not share them with the general education teacher.

Answer:

QUESTION 239

A special education teacher is designing a classroom environment for deaf students. Which modification is most likely to maximize visual learning opportunities in the classroom?

   A.   Installing soundproof walls to reduce noise.
   B.   Using bright, glare-free lighting to improve visibility.
   C.   Providing auditory simulations to enhance listening skills.
   D.   Increasing background noise to promote auditory attention.

Answer:

QUESTION 240

A special education teacher is working with a class of deaf and hard of hearing students. What classroom management strategy can help optimize transitions between lessons or classes for these students?

   A.   Minimize visual aids to avoid distractions during transitions.
   B.   Use spoken instructions for transitions to maintain consistency.
   C.   Implement a visual schedule with clear cues for transitions.
   D.   Allow students to choose their own transition times.

Answer:

QUESTION 241

A special education teacher is designing a classroom for deaf students. What technology adaptation is essential to enhance auditory learning opportunities?

   A.   High-intensity lighting for improved visibility.
   B.   Large, colorful posters for visual engagement.
   C.   Induction loop systems for hearing aid compatibility.
   D.   Text-only materials to minimize distractions.

Answer:

QUESTION 242

A special education teacher is managing a class of deaf and hard of hearing students. What classroom management strategy can help optimize instructional time and minimize disruptions?

   A.   Encourage students to engage in frequent verbal discussions.
   B.   Allow students to decide when to transition between tasks.
   C.   Establish clear expectations and routines for classroom behavior.
   D.   Provide students with individualized schedules to follow.

Answer:

QUESTION 243

A special education teacher is creating an inclusive classroom environment for both deaf and hearing students. What modification can enhance visual learning for all students in the classroom?

    A.   Use a traditional chalkboard for lessons.
    B.   Provide written transcripts of all spoken instructions.
    C.   Implement sign language as the primary mode of communication.
    D.   Incorporate auditory simulations for hearing students.

Answer:

QUESTION 244

A special education teacher is facing challenges with transitions between lessons in a class of deaf and hard of hearing students. What is a key strategy to facilitate smooth transitions?

    A.   Allow students to choose the duration of transitions.
    B.   Use only auditory cues to signal transitions.
    C.   Establish a visual schedule with clear time frames.
    D.   Minimize structure to promote flexibility.

Answer:

QUESTION 245

A special education teacher is working with a deaf student who has mastered a particular skill in the classroom but struggles to apply it outside of the classroom. What strategy is most effective for helping the student generalize this skill to various settings?

    A.   Limit practice to the classroom to ensure consistency.
    B.   Encourage the student to use the skill in real-world contexts.
    C.   Provide rewards only when the skill is used in the classroom.
    D.   Avoid discussing the skill outside of the classroom.

Answer:

QUESTION 246

A deaf high school student is struggling with time management and organization. What strategy can the special education teacher use to teach the student effective time management and organizational skills?

    A.   Provide step-by-step written instructions for organizing tasks.
    B.   Complete tasks for the student to demonstrate organization.
    C.   Assign additional homework to practice time management.
    D.   Encourage the student to set personal goals and develop a schedule.

Answer:

QUESTION 247

A deaf student has achieved excellent communication skills in the school environment but struggles to use them effectively at home. What can the special education teacher do to support the student's skill generalization?

    A.   Discourage the student from using sign language at home.
    B.   Provide isolated practice of communication skills only at school.
    C.   Collaborate with the student's family to reinforce communication skills at home.
    D.   Focus exclusively on communication skills in the school environment.

Answer:

QUESTION 248

A deaf student often struggles with understanding complex instructions in the classroom. What metacognitive strategy can the special education teacher teach the student to improve comprehension?

    A. Encourage the student to avoid asking for clarification.
    B. Teach the student to break down instructions into smaller steps.
    C. Discourage the student from seeking help.
    D. Provide all instructions in written form only.

Answer:

QUESTION 249

A deaf student consistently performs well in a specific learning environment but struggles to apply the same skills in other contexts. What approach can the special education teacher use to address this challenge?

    A. Focus on increasing the student's performance within the preferred learning environment.
    B. Encourage the student to avoid unfamiliar learning environments.
    C. Create opportunities for the student to practice skills in various settings.
    D. Isolate the student from unfamiliar learning environments.

Answer:

QUESTION 250

A deaf high school student is struggling with self-advocacy and often feels overwhelmed in noisy classroom settings. What strategy can the special education teacher teach the student to improve self-advocacy and address this challenge?

    A. Encourage the student to avoid discussing their needs with teachers.
    B. Teach the student to seek quiet spaces during noisy times.
    C. Discourage the student from self-advocacy.
    D. Provide hearing aids to eliminate noise challenges.

Answer:

QUESTION 251

A special education teacher is working with a deaf student who primarily uses American Sign Language (ASL) as their first language. The teacher is planning a lesson to teach English vocabulary to the student. What strategy is most appropriate for facilitating vocabulary acquisition in this context?

    A. Use only written materials in English to introduce vocabulary.
    B. Teach vocabulary exclusively through spoken English.
    C. Incorporate ASL signs alongside English vocabulary to support comprehension.
    D. Discourage the use of ASL during English lessons to avoid confusion.

Answer:

QUESTION 252

A special education teacher is working with a group of deaf students to improve their reading comprehension skills. What evidence-based strategy is most effective for developing reading comprehension in deaf or hard of hearing students?

    A. Rely on lip-reading to enhance comprehension.
    B. Focus exclusively on decoding skills without comprehension.
    C. Teach comprehension strategies such as making predictions, summarizing, and ing.
    D. Avoid discussions about reading comprehension to prevent confusion.

Answer:

QUESTION 253

A deaf student who is bilingual in both American Sign Language (ASL) and English is struggling to transfer writing skills from ASL to written English. What strategy can help facilitate this transfer of writing skills effectively?

A. Encourage the student to rely solely on ASL for writing practice.
B. Provide writing exercises only in ASL to maintain consistency.
C. Teach explicit strategies for transferring ASL writing skills to English writing.
D. Discourage the use of ASL writing altogether to avoid confusion.

Answer:

QUESTION 254

A special education teacher is working with a group of deaf students who are in the process of learning English as their second language. What approach should the teacher consider when teaching English grammar and syntax?

A. Rely on students' first language (e.g., ASL) grammar rules for English.
B. Avoid discussing grammar and syntax to prevent confusion.
C. Provide explicit instruction on English grammar rules and structures.
D. Teach grammar exclusively through spoken English.

Answer:

QUESTION 255

A special education teacher is working with a deaf student who struggles with reading fluency. What evidence-based strategy is most effective for improving reading fluency in this student?

A. Focusing solely on reading comprehension without addressing fluency.
B. Encouraging the student to read silently to improve fluency.
C. Implementing repeated oral reading of texts with appropriate feedback.
D. Avoiding reading practice to prevent frustration.

Answer:

QUESTION 256

A special education teacher is working with a deaf student who is proficient in both ASL and English but faces challenges when transferring written language skills between the two languages. What instructional approach is most effective for facilitating this transfer?

A. Discourage the use of ASL in writing to maintain English-only practice.
B. Teach writing skills in ASL and avoid written English.
C. Provide explicit instruction on how to transfer ASL writing skills to written English.
D. Focus on English writing exclusively and avoid discussing ASL writing.

Answer:

QUESTION 257

A high school student who is deaf is interested in connecting with the Deaf community and vocational rehabilitation services. What is the most appropriate strategy for teaching the student how to initiate contact with these resources?

A. Assume the responsibility for contacting these resources on behalf of the student.
B. Provide the student with contact information and encourage them to reach out independently.
C. Discourage the student from seeking external resources to focus on schoolwork.
D. Keep the student isolated from external resources to maintain control.

Answer

QUESTION 258

A deaf student is struggling to effectively communicate with their educational interpreter during classroom lessons. What strategy should the special education teacher employ to help the student use the interpreter more effectively?

    A.   Avoid discussing communication challenges to prevent embarrassment.
    B.   Encourage the student to rely solely on written communication.
    C.   Facilitate regular meetings between the student, interpreter, and teacher to discuss communication preferences and needs.
    D.   Discontinue the use of the educational interpreter to minimize confusion.

Answer:

QUESTION 259

A deaf student is transitioning from a sign language interpreter to a speech-to-text interpreter for certain classes. What should the special education teacher do to help the student adapt to this change effectively?

    A.   Avoid discussing the transition to prevent confusion.
    B.   Provide no support, expecting the student to adapt independently.
    C.   Facilitate a meeting to explain the transition and provide guidance on working with the new interpreter.
    D.   Discourage the use of interpreters altogether.

Answer:

QUESTION 260

A middle school student who is hard of hearing needs access to relay services but is unsure how to use them. What approach should the special education teacher take to teach the student to use relay services effectively?

    A.   Keep the student unaware of relay services to avoid confusion.
    B.   Provide written materials about relay services but no further guidance.
    C.   Offer hands-on guidance and practice in using relay services.
    D.   Discourage the use of relay services and rely on other communication methods.

Answer:

QUESTION 261

A high school student who is deaf has been provided with an educational interpreter but is not using them effectively during classes. What strategy should the special education teacher employ to address this issue?

    A.   Remove the educational interpreter to minimize distractions.
    B.   Keep the issue confidential and avoid discussing it with the student.
    C.   Facilitate a meeting involving the student, interpreter, and teacher to address communication challenges and preferences.
    D.   Encourage the student to rely solely on written materials for instruction.

Answer:

QUESTION 262

A deaf student is transitioning from using a sign language interpreter to a speech-to-text interpreter for specific classes. How can the special education teacher help the student adapt to this transition effectively?

    A.   Avoid discussing the transition to prevent confusion.
    B.   Provide written information about the new interpreter but no further guidance.
    C.   Offer training and practice sessions with the new speech-to-text interpreter.
    D.   Discourage the use of any interpreter and suggest self-reliance.

Answer:

QUESTION 263

A special education teacher is working with a deaf student's parents who want to be actively involved in their child's Individualized Education Program (IEP) development. What is the most effective strategy for involving the parents in the IEP process?

    A.   Exclude parents from IEP meetings to ensure professionalism.
    B.   Invite parents to IEP meetings but limit their participation.
    C.   Encourage parents to share their insights, concerns, and goals for their child.
    D.   Discourage parents from attending IEP meetings to avoid conflicts.

Answer:

QUESTION 264

A special education teacher is working with a culturally diverse group of families of deaf or hard of hearing students. What approach is most culturally responsive for ensuring effective communication and collaboration among these families, professionals, and community agencies?

    A.   Standardize communication methods to maintain consistency.
    B.   Avoid addressing cultural diversity to prevent misunderstandings.
    C.   Acknowledge and respect cultural differences, adapting communication as needed.
    D.   Isolate families from community agencies to minimize conflicts.

Answer:

QUESTION 265

A special education teacher is facing challenges in involving a deaf student's parents in the IEP process due to language barriers. What is the most effective strategy to address this issue and ensure their active participation?

    A.   Exclude the parents from IEP meetings to prevent language barriers.
    B.   Provide written IEP documents and expect parents to understand independently.
    C.   Arrange for qualified interpreters or bilingual professionals to facilitate communication.
    D.   Discourage the parents from attending IEP meetings to avoid language-related challenges.

Answer:

QUESTION 266

A special education teacher is working with a culturally diverse group of families, some of whom have different beliefs about disability and education. What approach should the teacher take to foster cultural responsiveness and effective collaboration among these families, professionals, and community agencies?

    A.   Standardize practices without consideration for cultural beliefs.
    B.   Avoid discussions about cultural beliefs to prevent conflicts.
    C.   Engage in open dialogue, respect diverse perspectives, and seek common ground.
    D.   Isolate families with different beliefs to minimize disagreements.

Answer:

QUESTION 267

A special education teacher is working with a deaf student's parents who are hesitant to participate in the IEP process due to previous negative experiences. What approach should the teacher take to encourage their active involvement and rebuild trust?

    A.   Exclude the parents from IEP meetings to avoid further negative experiences.
    B.   Provide limited opportunities for participation to minimize potential conflicts.
    C.   Create a welcoming and supportive environment, addressing their concerns and involving them in decision-making.
    D.   Discourage the parents from attending IEP meetings to prevent potential conflicts.

Answer:

QUESTION 268

A special education teacher is researching the historical foundations of deaf education. Which historical figure is most closely associated with advocating for manual communication methods, such as sign language, as an instructional approach for deaf individuals?

    A. Alexander Graham Bell
    B. Thomas Hopkins Gallaudet
    C. Jean-Marc Gaspard Itard
    D. Helen Keller

Answer:

QUESTION 269

What term is commonly used in educational contexts to describe a degree of hearing loss that ranges from mild to profound, and typically involves the use of hearing aids or assistive listening devices?

    A. Deafness
    B. Profound deafness
    C. Mild hearing loss
    D. Moderate hearing loss

Answer:

QUESTION 270

In the history of deaf education, which influential educator and advocate established the first permanent public school for the deaf in the United States and promoted the use of sign language as the primary mode of communication for deaf students?

    A. Alexander Graham Bell
    B. Laurent Clerc
    C. Samuel Gridley Howe
    D. Marie Jean Philibert

Answer:

QUESTION 271

In educational terminology, what is the term used to describe a person who has a hearing loss but primarily communicates through spoken language, often with the support of hearing aids or cochlear implants?

    A. Deaf
    B. Profoundly Deaf
    C. Hard of Hearing
    D. Mild Hearing Loss

Answer:

QUESTION 272

Which philosophical perspective in deaf education emphasizes the importance of fostering a strong Deaf cultural identity and using sign language as a primary mode of communication?

    A. Auditory-Oral Approach
    B. Mainstreaming Philosophy
    C. Total Communication Philosophy
    D. Bicultural-Bilingual Approach

Answer:

QUESTION 273

In educational contexts, what term is used to describe a hearing loss that is present at birth or acquired early in life, often before the development of spoken language skills?

A. Congenital hearing loss
B. Acquired hearing loss
C. Sensorineural hearing loss
D. Conductive hearing loss

Answer:

QUESTION 274

A special education teacher is faced with a challenging situation involving a student who is deaf and their family. The teacher believes that following the CEC Code of Ethics is essential. What principle from the CEC Code of Ethics should guide the teacher's actions in this situation?

A. Prioritize personal beliefs over the best interests of the student.
B. Advocate for the student's rights and well-being while respecting confidentiality.
C. Avoid involving parents in the decision-making process.
D. Disregard the needs and preferences of the student.

Answer:

QUESTION 275

A special education teacher is planning an inclusive classroom environment for students who are deaf or hard of hearing. What should be the primary consideration when designing the classroom to ensure compliance with applicable laws and policies?

A. Exclude students with hearing loss to simplify compliance.
B. Prioritize the needs of students without hearing loss.
C. Ensure equal access and accommodations for all students.
D. Disregard individualized needs to streamline compliance efforts.

Answer:

QUESTION 276

A special education teacher is involved in a dispute with colleagues regarding the appropriate placement of a deaf student. How can the teacher ensure that their actions align with the CEC Code of Ethics during this disagreement?

A. Avoid discussing the disagreement with colleagues to prevent conflict.
B. Advocate for the placement the teacher believes is best for the student while respecting the perspectives of colleagues.
C. Exclude the deaf student from the decision-making process to simplify matters.
D. Prioritize the teacher's perspective over colleagues' opinions.

Answer:

QUESTION 277

A special education teacher is responsible for ensuring that students who are deaf or hard of hearing receive appropriate accommodations in standardized testing. What should be the teacher's primary focus when implementing accommodations to ensure compliance with testing policies?

A. Overlook accommodations to maintain test integrity.
B. Provide accommodations that may give students an unfair advantage.
C. Ensure that accommodations meet the specific needs of each student while adhering to testing policies.
D. Disregard the testing policies to prioritize student comfort.

Answer:

QUESTION 278

A special education teacher has concerns about a colleague's practices that may be in violation of ethical standards. What is the most appropriate action for the teacher to take in this situation, in accordance with the CEC Code of Ethics?

    A. Ignore the concerns to avoid conflicts with the colleague.
    B. Report the concerns to the principal without discussing them with the colleague.
    C. Address the concerns directly with the colleague while maintaining confidentiality.
    D. Share the concerns with other colleagues to gather their opinions before taking action.

Answer:

QUESTION 279

A special education teacher is responsible for ensuring that a student who is deaf receives appropriate communication accommodations in the classroom. What should be the teacher's primary objective when implementing these accommodations to ensure compliance with legal requirements?

    A. Disregard individualized needs to streamline the process.
    B. Provide accommodations only when requested by the student.
    C. Ensure that communication accommodations effectively support the student's learning and participation.
    D. Exclude the student from the classroom to avoid compliance challenges.

Answer:

QUESTION 280

Which part of the ear is responsible for converting sound waves into electrical signals that are sent to the brain?

    A. Cochlea
    B. Eardrum
    C. Ossicles
    D. Auditory nerve

Answer:

QUESTION 281

In a classroom, a student who is hard of hearing often struggles to understand speech when there is background noise. Which part of the auditory system is most likely contributing to this difficulty?

    A. Outer ear
    B. Middle ear
    C. Inner ear
    D. Auditory processing centers in the brain

Answer:

QUESTION 282

A young child with a hearing impairment shows difficulty localizing the source of a sound. Which part of the auditory system is likely affected?

    A. Outer ear
    B. Middle ear
    C. Inner ear
    D. Auditory cortex in the brain

Answer:

QUESTION 283

During a hearing assessment, a student with a hearing impairment displays a type of hearing loss where they can hear low-frequency sounds but have difficulty hearing high-frequency sounds. Which part of the auditory system is likely affected?

A. Cochlea
B. Ossicles
C. Auditory nerve
D. Auditory cortex in the brain

Answer:

QUESTION 284

A child with a hearing impairment has been using a cochlear implant. What part of the auditory system is bypassed or replaced by this device?

A. Ossicles
B. Inner ear
C. Auditory nerve
D. Auditory cortex in the brain

Answer:

QUESTION 285

In the process of typical auditory development, which skill is usually the first to develop in infants?

A. Sound localization
B. Discrimination of speech sounds
C. Startle response to loud noises
D. Ability to hear faint sounds

Answer:

QUESTION 286

In a classroom, a student who is both deaf and has a learning disability is struggling to grasp written instructions. Which teaching strategy would be most effective in this situation?

A. Providing visual aids and demonstrations
B. Using written instructions supplemented with sign language
C. Assigning additional reading materials for practice
D. Conducting regular oral assessments

Answer:

QUESTION 287

A student who is deaf and also has attention deficit hyperactivity disorder (ADHD) tends to become easily distracted during group activities. What modification can best support their learning?

A. Assigning individual tasks to complete
B. Increasing the volume of instructions
C. Encouraging participation in more group activities
D. Providing additional written assignments

Answer:

QUESTION 288

A student who is deaf and has autism spectrum disorder (ASD) displays sensitivity to sensory stimuli, including auditory input. How might this impact their learning in a typical classroom setting?

A. They may become overwhelmed or anxious in noisy environments.
B. They may excel in activities requiring auditory processing.
C. They may struggle with visual tasks.
D. They may have difficulty forming social connections.

Answer:

QUESTION 289

A student with a hearing impairment and intellectual disability has difficulty with expressive language skills. What teaching strategy would be most beneficial for promoting their communication?

A. Utilizing augmentative and alternative communication (AAC) devices
B. Encouraging verbal communication without aids
C. Providing written materials only
D. Focusing exclusively on receptive language skills

Answer:

QUESTION 290

In a scenario where a student with a hearing impairment also experiences mobility challenges, how might their learning environment need to be adapted?

A. Providing accessible seating and workstations
B. Increasing the amount of verbal instruction
C. Offering additional physical education classes
D. Encouraging participation in team sports

Answer:

QUESTION 291

In a classroom with a student who is deaf and has dyslexia, what modification can be implemented to facilitate their reading skills?

A. Providing text-to-speech software
B. Assigning more written assignments
C. Conducting additional oral assessments
D. Increasing the font size of written materials

Answer:

QUESTION 292

In the context of assessments for students who are deaf or hard of hearing, what does the term "auditory discrimination" refer to?

A. The ability to identify and distinguish between different speech sounds.
B. The process of conducting hearing tests to determine the degree of hearing loss.
C. Assessing a student's ability to comprehend written text.
D. Evaluating a student's proficiency in sign language.

Answer:

QUESTION 293

A student who is hard of hearing performs well in informal conversational settings but struggles during formal assessments. What could be a potential limitation of formal assessments for this student?

    A.   They may not accurately reflect the student's true communication abilities.
    B.   They may require specialized equipment that the school does not have.
    C.   They may not be administered by qualified professionals.
    D.   They may not be suitable for assessing students with hearing impairments.

Answer:

QUESTION 294

When assessing a student who is deaf for speech development, what is an appropriate specialized terminology used to describe the ability to produce speech sounds accurately?

    A.   Articulation
    B.   Phonics
    C.   Morphology
    D.   Syntax

Answer:

QUESTION 295

In a scenario where a student is deaf and also has a cognitive disability, which type of assessment might be most effective in understanding their overall learning needs?

    A.   Functional behavior assessment
    B.   Norm-referenced achievement test
    C.   Curriculum-based assessment
    D.   Dynamic assessment

Answer:

QUESTION 296

In the assessment of a student who is deaf, why is it important to consider their preferred mode of communication?

    A.   It ensures that the assessment is administered by a qualified professional.
    B.   It helps determine if the student has a learning disability.
    C.   It allows for fair and accurate evaluation of the student's abilities.
    D.   It determines the degree of hearing loss.

Answer:

QUESTION 297

In the assessment of a student who is hard of hearing, what is an example of an informal assessment that can provide valuable insights into their language development?

    A.   Language sample analysis
    B.   Standardized receptive vocabulary test
    C.   Pure-tone audiometry
    D.   Speech-in-noise testing

Answer:

QUESTION 298

Jane is a 12-year-old student who is deaf. She uses sign language as her primary mode of communication and is proficient in reading and writing in English. During a recent assessment, Jane's results on a standardized reading comprehension test were significantly below grade level. The test was administered in a written format. What should the special education teacher consider when interpreting Jane's performance on the standardized reading comprehension test?

    A.   Jane's results accurately reflect her reading comprehension skills.
    B.   The test format may not have been accessible for Jane due to her deafness.
    C.   Jane's English proficiency may not be at grade level.
    D.   Jane's sign language skills need improvement.

Answer:

QUESTION 299

Mark, a 15-year-old student who is hard of hearing, has been receiving speech therapy services to improve his articulation skills. The speech therapist administers a formal assessment that measures Mark's articulation accuracy in English words and sentences. What is a limitation of using a formal articulation assessment for Mark, considering his hearing impairment?

    A.   The assessment may not accurately represent Mark's articulation skills.
    B.   Mark's hearing loss will not impact his articulation abilities.
    C.   Formal assessments are always the most accurate way to assess articulation.
    D.   The assessment will identify any cognitive disabilities Mark may have.

Answer:

QUESTION 300

Sarah, a 10-year-old student who is deaf, recently underwent a formal standardized assessment of her mathematical abilities. The results indicate that she is performing significantly below her grade level in mathematics. What additional information should the special education teacher consider when interpreting Sarah's assessment results?

    A.   Sarah's hearing loss is the sole factor affecting her mathematical abilities.
    B.   Sarah's preferred mode of communication and accommodations during the assessment.
    C.   Sarah's overall intelligence level.
    D.   The teacher's own assessment of Sarah's mathematical skills.

Answer:

QUESTION 301

Sarah, a 7-year-old student who is deaf, recently underwent an audiogram assessment. The results indicate a moderate hearing loss in her left ear and a severe hearing loss in her right ear. Sarah's parents are concerned about her academic progress. As a special education teacher, how would you interpret the audiogram results to Sarah's parents and explain their potential impact on her learning?

    A.   Emphasize the need for hearing aids for both ears to correct the hearing loss.
    B.   Explain that the hearing loss may affect her ability to hear sounds on the right side.
    C.   Highlight the potential impact on speech and language development and recommend appropriate interventions.
    D.   Suggest cochlear implant surgery to address the severe hearing loss.

Answer:

QUESTION 302

Alex, a teenager who is hard of hearing, recently completed a speech reception threshold assessment. The results show that he has difficulty understanding speech in noisy environments, even with hearing aids. How would you communicate the results of the speech reception threshold assessment to Alex's teachers, and what strategies might you recommend to support his classroom participation?

    A.   Share the assessment results and recommend using hearing protection in noisy environments.
    B.   Explain that Alex needs to improve his hearing aid settings to enhance his speech understanding.
    C.   Provide information on Alex's difficulty in noisy settings and suggest preferential seating or the use of FM systems.
    D.   Recommend that Alex avoids noisy environments to prevent further hearing loss.

Answer:

QUESTION 303

Emma, a 6-year-old student who is deaf, has undergone an articulation assessment. The results indicate age-appropriate articulation skills. How would you communicate the results of Emma's articulation assessment to her parents, and what strategies might you recommend for continued speech development?

    A.   Share the assessment results and suggest no further action is needed.
    B.   Explain that Emma's speech is age-appropriate, but regular speech therapy can enhance her skills.
    C.   Emphasize that Emma needs immediate speech therapy to correct her articulation difficulties.
    D.   Recommend sign language instruction as speech therapy is not effective for deaf students.

Answer:

QUESTION 304

James, a high school student who is deaf, recently had a comprehensive assessment of his auditory processing skills. The results show below-average auditory processing abilities. How would you convey the results of James' auditory processing assessment to his general education teachers and recommend strategies to support his learning in a mainstream classroom?

    A.   Share the assessment results and recommend that James sit closer to the front of the classroom.
    B.   Explain that the assessment results indicate below-average auditory processing skills and suggest using visual aids and captioned materials.
    C.   Emphasize the need for hearing aids to improve auditory processing.
    D.   Recommend that James be placed in a specialized deaf education classroom.

Answer:

QUESTION 305

Sophia, a 9-year-old student who is deaf, recently completed a comprehensive speech assessment. The results show that she has made significant progress in her articulation skills. How would you share the positive results of Sophia's speech assessment with her parents and teachers, and what strategies might you recommend for continued speech development?

    A.   Share the assessment results and recommend immediate discontinuation of speech therapy.
    B.   Explain that Sophia's speech has improved significantly and suggest periodic monitoring to ensure continued progress.
    C.   Emphasize that Sophia needs more intensive speech therapy to maintain her current level of progress.
    D.   Recommend that Sophia switch to a different mode of communication as speech therapy is not effective.

Answer:

QUESTION 306

Nathan, a 14-year-old student who is hard of hearing, recently had an assessment of his auditory processing abilities. The results indicate that he struggles with processing rapid speech and complex auditory information. How would you communicate the assessment results to Nathan's parents and teachers, and what strategies might you recommend to support his auditory processing difficulties in the classroom?

A. Share the assessment results and suggest using hearing protection in noisy environments.
B. Explain that Nathan's hearing aids need adjustment to improve auditory processing.
C. Emphasize the need for Nathan to sit closer to the front of the classroom.
D. Recommend the use of auditory processing therapy and preferential seating in the classroom.

Answer:

QUESTION 307

Maria is a 10-year-old student who is deaf and comes from a culturally diverse background. She uses a combination of sign language and spoken English to communicate. Her recent assessments indicate that she excels in mathematics but struggles with written English. Considering Maria's assessment results, what program and service delivery decisions might be most beneficial for her?

A. Enrolling Maria in a bilingual education program that supports both sign language and written English.
B. Placing Maria in a specialized program exclusively focused on sign language instruction.
C. Recommending additional mathematics instruction to further excel in her strengths.
D. Suggesting a mainstream classroom placement without additional supports.

Answer:

QUESTION 308

Ethan is a 13-year-old student who is hard of hearing with additional learning challenges. He excels in hands-on activities and benefits from visual learning materials. His recent assessments indicate a need for additional support in reading comprehension. Considering Ethan's learning profile, what educational placement option might be most effective for him?

A. Enrolling Ethan in a specialized program that emphasizes hands-on learning and incorporates visual materials.
B. Placing Ethan in a general education classroom without additional supports.
C. Recommending intensive one-on-one tutoring for reading comprehension.
D. Suggesting placement in a program for students with cognitive disabilities.

Answer:

QUESTION 309

Raj, a 16-year-old student who is deaf, is highly proficient in American Sign Language (ASL) and has strong academic skills. His assessments indicate above-average performance in both mathematics and science. What educational placement option might be most suitable for Raj?

A. Placing Raj in a mainstream classroom with appropriate supports for his deafness and providing advanced coursework in mathematics and science.
B. Recommending placement in a specialized program exclusively focused on sign language instruction.
C. Enrolling Raj in a vocational program to develop practical skills.
D. Suggesting a self-contained classroom for students with hearing impairments.

Answer:

QUESTION 310

Aisha, a 9-year-old student who is deaf, comes from a culturally and linguistically diverse background. Her assessments show that she excels in expressive sign language skills but struggles with written English. What program and service delivery decisions might best support Aisha's educational needs?

    A.   Providing specialized instruction that builds on her expressive sign language skills and offers support for written English.
    B.   Placing Aisha in a mainstream classroom without additional supports.
    C.   Recommending additional English language instruction without considering her sign language skills.
    D.   Enrolling Aisha in an exclusive program focused solely on written English.

Answer:

QUESTION 311

Omar, a 12-year-old student who is hard of hearing, is an avid artist with a strong interest in visual arts. His assessments show proficiency in art but a need for additional support in language arts. What educational placement option might be most effective for Omar?

    A.   Placing Omar in a general education classroom and providing additional support for language arts, while encouraging his passion for visual arts.
    B.   Enrolling Omar in a specialized program exclusively focused on visual arts.
    C.   Recommending placement in a program for students with learning disabilities.
    D.   Suggesting a self-contained classroom for students with hearing impairments.

Answer:

QUESTION 312

Leila, a 14-year-old student who is deaf, is highly motivated and academically inclined. Her assessments indicate above-average performance in all subjects. What educational placement option might be most suitable for Leila?

    A.   Placing Leila in a mainstream classroom with appropriate supports for her deafness and providing opportunities for advanced coursework.
    B.   Recommending placement in a specialized program exclusively focused on sign language instruction.
    C.   Enrolling Leila in a vocational program to develop practical skills.
    D.   Suggesting a self-contained classroom for students with hearing impairments.

Answer:

QUESTION 313

Alex is a 9-year-old student who is deaf and comes from a culturally and linguistically diverse background. He primarily communicates using American Sign Language (ASL) and is in a mainstream classroom with appropriate supports. Alex's recent assessments show that he excels in mathematics but struggles with written English. Given Alex's assessment results and background, what recommendations might you make for his educational program, placement, and services?

    A.   Suggest a bilingual education program that emphasizes both ASL and written English, along with continued support in mathematics.
    B.   Recommend transitioning Alex to a specialized program exclusively focused on sign language instruction.
    C.   Advocate for a self-contained classroom for students with hearing impairments without additional services in mathematics.
    D.   Propose a mainstream classroom placement without additional supports.

Answer:

QUESTION 314

Sophie is a 14-year-old student who is hard of hearing and comes from a culturally and linguistically diverse background. She uses a combination of speech and hearing aids to communicate. Sophie's recent assessments indicate that she excels in science but requires additional support in English language arts. Considering Sophie's assessment results and background, what educational placement options might be most effective for her?

    A.   Enroll Sophie in a mainstream classroom with appropriate supports for her hearing loss, and provide additional support in English language arts while offering advanced coursework in science.

    B.   Place Sophie in a specialized program exclusively focused on speech therapy to improve her language arts skills.

    C.   Suggest a self-contained classroom for students with hearing impairments without additional services in science.

    D.   Recommend placement in a general education classroom without additional supports.

Answer:

QUESTION 315

Jaden is a 14-year-old student who is deaf. He is part of a close-knit community where privacy is highly valued. Jaden's parents have expressed concerns about the confidentiality of his educational records. What is a critical step for Jaden's teacher in ensuring the confidentiality of his educational records while respecting his community's values?

    A.   Establishing clear protocols for storing and accessing Jaden's records, ensuring that only authorized personnel have access.

    B.   Sharing Jaden's records with the entire community to promote transparency.

    C.   Avoiding documentation altogether to align with the community's values.

    D.   Providing complete access to Jaden's records to anyone who requests it, regardless of authorization.

Answer:

QUESTION 316

Olivia is a 12-year-old student who is deaf. She has recently expressed a strong interest in being more involved in decisions regarding her educational plan, including the management of her records. What is an appropriate step for Olivia's teacher to take in response to her desire for increased involvement in managing her educational records?

    A.   Collaborating with Olivia to provide her with guidance on how to request and review her records, empowering her to take an active role in the process.

    B.   Discouraging Olivia from getting involved in managing her records to avoid potential complications.

    C.   Assuming full responsibility for managing Olivia's records without involving her in the process.

    D.   Denying Olivia access to her records due to her age and suggesting that her parents handle all matters related to her educational plan.

Answer:

Chapter 2 – Answers and Explanations

QUESTION 1

Answer: B

Explanation: This strategy promotes social interaction and communication with peers, which can help mitigate frustration and improve the student's classroom experience. It encourages inclusion and supports the student's social and educational development.

QUESTION 2

Answer: C

Explanation: It's important to support the student's aspirations and explore ways to accommodate their hearing impairment, such as using assistive technology or working with theater companies that are inclusive and accommodating of their needs.

QUESTION 3

Answer: B

Explanation: Side effects such as dizziness and fatigue can hinder a student's ability to concentrate and engage in learning activities. Special accommodations may be needed to address these challenges.

QUESTION 4

Answer: B

Explanation: It's essential to assess the student's learning strengths and challenges accurately, especially when multiple factors like hearing impairment and a potential learning disability are involved. This assessment will help tailor appropriate interventions and support.

QUESTION 5

Answer: B

Explanation: It's essential to work collaboratively with healthcare providers to explore possible accommodations or adjustments to the medication regimen that can minimize side effects while allowing the student to continue their education.

QUESTION 6

Answer: C

Explanation: Creating an inclusive and supportive classroom where the student feels understood and accepted can help address emotional and behavioral challenges. Isolation and switching to a specialized school should be considered only after other supportive measures have been attempted and evaluated.

QUESTION 7

Answer: C

Explanation: This option focuses on addressing Sarah's communication challenges while still allowing her to pursue her passion for science. Working with a speech-language therapist can help develop effective communication strategies and support her career aspirations.

QUESTION 8

Answer: B

Explanation: This option acknowledges Alex's hearing difficulties and provides a reasonable accommodation to help him perform better academically. Transferring to a specialized school or repeating a grade should be considered only after trying appropriate accommodations and interventions.

QUESTION 9

Answer: B

Explanation: This option recognizes the importance of addressing Daniel's emotional well-being and social isolation. Group counseling sessions can provide a supportive and understanding environment where students can share their experiences and learn coping strategies. Isolation or switching schools should be considered only after other supportive measures have been explored and evaluated.

QUESTION 10

Answer: B

Explanation: Early exposure to sign language can support language development in children with hearing loss, even if they eventually receive cochlear implants or hearing aids. It is essential to begin intervention early to maximize language acquisition.

QUESTION 11

Answer: C

Explanation: It's crucial to ensure that the student receives appropriate accommodations, such as preferential seating, captioning, or the use of assistive listening devices, to facilitate their access to spoken instructions and classroom discussions.

QUESTION 12

Answer: C

Explanation: It is essential to provide information and guidance on safety precautions and the appropriate sports equipment to minimize risks while allowing the student to pursue their interests in sports.

QUESTION 13

Answer: C

Explanation: Emotional challenges can arise during therapy sessions, especially for young children adjusting to cochlear implants. Providing emotional support and encouragement can help build confidence and resilience as they adapt to this new experience.

QUESTION 14

Answer: C

Explanation: Vibrating platforms can provide tactile feedback, allowing the student to feel the music's rhythm and vibrations, making it more accessible for individuals with hearing loss. It's important to explore and implement such accommodations to support their musical pursuits.

QUESTION 15

Answer: B

Explanation: It's important to assess and explore appropriate assistive technology options that can enhance communication and mobility for the student. Enrolling in a specialized school or withdrawing from social interactions should be considered only after trying supportive measures and assistive technologies.

QUESTION 16

Answer: B

Explanation: This approach allows Mia to review the content beforehand, which can enhance her participation and comprehension during group discussions. It supports inclusive learning while acknowledging her primary mode of communication.

QUESTION 17

Answer: B

Explanation: For students like Max, taking breaks can help prevent auditory fatigue and maintain attention. Extending lecture duration or sitting in the back of the classroom may not be effective strategies and could potentially worsen the situation.

QUESTION 18

Answer: B

Explanation: Encouraging Ben to explore coding and programming languages aligns with his career aspirations and offers a practical way to support his interests. Discouraging or recommending a career change should not be the first response.

QUESTION 19

Answer: B

Explanation: Speech therapy that emphasizes auditory and oral skills can help improve Sarah's speech and language development, which is particularly important if she is using a cochlear implant. Relying solely on sign language or switching to a specialized school may not address her specific needs.

QUESTION 20

Answer: B

Explanation: It's important to offer targeted support to help Alex improve his skills in English language arts while continuing to excel in mathematics. Encouraging a well-rounded education is essential for his overall development.

QUESTION 21

Answer: B

Explanation: Utilizing visual aids and multimedia presentations can make the science fair presentation more accessible and inclusive for all students, including those who are deaf or hard of hearing. Requiring spoken language only or canceling the presentation would not promote inclusivity.

QUESTION 22

Answer: B

Explanation: Multisensory instruction, which engages multiple senses, can enhance cognitive development in deaf and hard of hearing students by providing different pathways for learning and understanding.

QUESTION 23

Answer: B

Explanation: Research suggests that exposing deaf students to auditory experiences, such as spoken language and environmental sounds, can positively influence their cognitive development. This intervention can help bridge the gap between sensory input and cognitive growth.

QUESTION 24

Answer: C

Explanation: Sign language can provide a rich and accessible way for deaf and hard of hearing students to acquire language and enhance cognitive development. It allows for meaningful communication and cognitive growth.

QUESTION 25

Answer: B

Explanation: Utilizing tactile and visual aids can provide essential sensory input that enhances the cognitive development of a deaf student in mathematics. These aids can help them grasp abstract mathematical concepts more effectively.

QUESTION 26

Answer: C

Explanation: Research should focus on how these sensory inputs impact the cognitive development of children who are deaf or hard of hearing. Understanding the interplay of these sensory modalities is crucial for informed educational practices.

QUESTION 27

Answer: C

Explanation: For a student struggling with language acquisition and cognitive development, incorporating visual and tactile experiences can provide alternative pathways for learning and understanding. This multisensory approach can be highly effective in supporting their cognitive growth.

QUESTION 28

Answer: C

Explanation: In Emily's case, using tactile and visual aids can provide additional sensory input to enhance her cognitive development. This approach aligns with research suggesting that multiple sensory inputs can be beneficial for deaf and hard of hearing students.

QUESTION 29

Answer: C

Explanation: For students like Sam, it's essential to provide auditory experiences that complement the cochlear implant. This approach can enhance language and cognitive development by utilizing the device while offering additional sensory input.

QUESTION 30

Answer: C

Explanation: The research finding suggests that incorporating multiple sensory inputs into instruction has a positive impact on the cognitive development of deaf and hard of hearing children. This conclusion underscores the importance of multisensory approaches in their education.

QUESTION 31

Answer: B

Explanation: The initial step in the screening and referral process should involve collaboration with parents to gain insights into Sarah's learning challenges. This partnership can help determine if further assessment for learning disabilities is warranted.

QUESTION 32

Answer: B

Explanation: Collaborating with the school's Child Study Team is the appropriate next step to conduct a comprehensive assessment of Alex's needs and determine if special education services are necessary. This team can provide expertise in the referral and evaluation process.

QUESTION 33

Answer: B

Explanation: When a student's performance on a standardized assessment is significantly lower than expected, it's essential to review the assessment administration process to ensure its accuracy before making any decisions about placement or interventions.

QUESTION 34

Answer: A

Explanation: Providing an interpreter who can sign the assessment s to Mia ensures that she can access the content in a way that aligns with her primary mode of communication. This modification supports her equitable participation in the assessment.

QUESTION 35

Answer: D

Explanation: It's essential to tailor assessment modifications to each student's specific needs and communication preferences. This approach ensures fair and accurate assessment results for all students in the group.

QUESTION 36

Answer: B

Explanation: Providing a scribe or assistive technology that supports Ben in recording his responses ensures that his motor difficulties do not hinder his participation in the assessment. This modification allows him to demonstrate his knowledge effectively.

QUESTION 37

Answer: B

Explanation: To support Jordan's ASL development, it's crucial to address their specific challenges, in this case, syntax. Individualized lessons can help improve their skills in this area while building on their strengths in morphology.

QUESTION 38

Answer: A

Explanation: Effective communication of assessment results includes providing a comprehensive overview, both strengths and weaknesses, to guide appropriate interventions. Recommending additional support demonstrates a commitment to addressing areas of concern.

QUESTION 39

Answer: B

Explanation: It is essential to emphasize the significance of balanced ASL skills. This understanding can motivate the student to work on improving their morphology while continuing to build on their strong semantics skills.

QUESTION 40

Answer: D

Explanation: To effectively communicate assessment results and encourage growth in ASL syntax, organizing group workshops can create a supportive and collaborative learning environment where students can work together to improve their skills. This approach fosters a sense of community and shared effort.

QUESTION 41

Answer: C

Explanation: Effective communication with parents involves transparency and providing a complete picture of a student's ASL skills. This approach allows for informed decision-making and collaboration in addressing Leo's needs.

QUESTION 42

Answer: C

Explanation: Group seminars can be an effective way to communicate assessment results and provide targeted instruction to address the shared challenge of ASL semantics. This approach fosters a supportive and collaborative learning environment for students to improve their skills.

QUESTION 43

Answer: C

Explanation: When developing a Communication Plan, it is essential to consider the individual student's needs, strengths, and preferences. Customizing the plan ensures that it aligns with Alex's specific requirements for effective communication.

QUESTION 44

Answer: B

Explanation: Special education goals for deaf and hard of hearing students should aim to provide access to the general education curriculum and align with the established standards. This approach ensures that students have meaningful educational experiences and opportunities for academic success.

QUESTION 45

Answer: C

Explanation: Effective Communication Plans should be personalized to address the specific needs and communication preferences of the individual student, like Mia, who may have unique requirements due to additional disabilities.

QUESTION 46

Answer: D

Explanation: The key to effective individualized learning goals for deaf and hard of hearing students is to tailor the sequence of goals to match each student's unique learning needs and abilities, ensuring meaningful progress.

QUESTION 47

Answer: B

Explanation: To meet the diverse needs of students with varying sign language proficiency levels, it is crucial to create individualized Communication Plans that align with their abilities and preferences. This approach ensures effective communication support.

QUESTION 48

Answer: C

Explanation: Long-term individualized learning goals for students like Ben should be tailored to their unique learning needs and abilities while also considering their potential for accessing the general education curriculum. This approach promotes meaningful educational progress.

QUESTION 49

Answer: A

Explanation: Deaf students often face challenges in understanding spoken language, especially in content-heavy subjects like math. Providing sign language support and visual aids can help bridge the communication gap and improve her understanding of math concepts.

QUESTION 50

Answer: C

Explanation: To cater to the diverse communication needs of deaf and hard of hearing students, it is essential to provide multiple options. Offering both sign language interpretation and written materials allows students to access the content in a way that aligns with their communication preferences.

QUESTION 51

Answer: C

Explanation: To accommodate varying degrees of hearing loss, it is essential to offer a combination of written materials and sign language support. This approach ensures that students can access the content effectively regardless of their hearing loss level.

QUESTION 52

Answer: B

Explanation: Deaf students, like David, may benefit from sign language support and visual aids to enhance their understanding of complex literary texts. These tools can help bridge the gap between written language and comprehension.

QUESTION 53

Answer: C

Explanation: To cater to the diverse communication needs of deaf and hard of hearing students in physical education, it is essential to provide both sign language interpretation and visual cues during activities. This ensures that all students can participate and understand the instructions.

QUESTION 54

Answer: C

Explanation: Assigning a peer note-taker can be an effective strategy to support Emily's learning by providing transcriptions of class lectures. This accommodation ensures that Emily has access to the content and can review it at her own pace.

QUESTION 55

Answer: B

Explanation: For a deaf student like Liam who primarily uses ASL, providing sign language support and visual aids can bridge the gap between ASL and written language, improving his reading comprehension.

QUESTION 56

Answer: C

Explanation: To effectively teach vocabulary to a group of diverse learners with varying communication preferences, offering both spoken and sign language instruction as options ensures that students can access the content in their preferred mode of communication.

QUESTION 57

Answer: C

Explanation: For a student like Ava who uses spoken language, providing explicit instruction in speech sounds and phonological awareness is an evidence-based strategy to address her difficulties in this area.

QUESTION 58

Answer: C

Explanation: For a student like Owen who primarily uses sign language, providing explicit instruction in written language skills is an evidence-based strategy to help him develop this important skill.

QUESTION 59

Answer: C

Explanation: To cater to the diverse communication needs of deaf and hard of hearing students in a reading class, offering both sign language interpretation and visual aids as options ensures that students can access the content in their preferred mode of communication.

QUESTION 60

Answer: C

Explanation: For a student like Maya who uses a combination of spoken language and sign language, a balanced approach that combines both modes of communication can support her language development effectively.

QUESTION 61

Answer: D

Explanation: To facilitate effective communication for Emily during drama club activities, it is beneficial to use a combination of sign language interpreters and visual cues to ensure she can fully participate and engage with her peers.

QUESTION 62

Answer: C

Explanation: To ensure that deaf and hard of hearing students can fully participate and benefit from the museum visit, providing visual aids and written materials can enhance their understanding of the exhibits and programs.

QUESTION 63

Answer: D

Explanation: To support effective communication between your students and community members during the community service project, using a combination of sign language interpreters and visual cues can facilitate meaningful interactions.

QUESTION 64

Answer: B

Explanation: To ensure effective communication for your students during the science fair, providing sign language interpreters for specific presentations and discussions can enable them to fully engage and understand the content.

QUESTION 65

Answer: D

Explanation: To facilitate effective communication between your students and other volunteers during the outdoor cleanup initiative, using a combination of visual cues and sign language interpreters can enhance interactions and ensure clarity in communication.

QUESTION 66

Answer: D

Explanation: To support effective communication between the bank representatives and your students during the financial literacy workshop, using a combination of sign language interpreters and visual aids can ensure that students have access to the content and can actively participate in the workshop.

QUESTION 67

Answer: B

Explanation: Inviting a Deaf guest speaker allows students to hear firsthand experiences and perspectives on Deaf history and culture, fostering a deeper understanding and connection.

QUESTION 68

Answer: C

Explanation: To prepare students for meaningful interactions with a Deaf community, offering cultural sensitivity training and basic sign language instruction equips them with the necessary skills and awareness to engage effectively.

QUESTION 69

Answer: C

Explanation: To ensure an inclusive and respectful Deaf History Month assembly, inviting Deaf individuals to perform sign language poetry allows for the celebration of Deaf culture and heritage through a medium deeply rooted in the community's artistic expression.

QUESTION 70

Answer: C

Explanation: To promote meaningful interactions and cultural understanding during the field trip, having guided tours led by Deaf cultural center staff allows students to engage with knowledgeable individuals who can share insights and experiences related to Deaf culture.

QUESTION 71

Answer: C

Explanation: Facilitating the involvement and interaction of deaf and hard of hearing students with the Deaf community is most effectively achieved by having sign language interpreters available to ensure clear communication and full participation.

QUESTION 72

Answer: B

Explanation: A sign language workshop allows participants to actively engage and learn how to communicate using a visual language, fostering meaningful interactions and mutual understanding with individuals who are deaf or hard of hearing.

QUESTION 73

Answer: C

Explanation: Collaborating with professionals through scheduled meetings allows for in-depth discussions and planning to ensure Ethan's successful participation in extracurricular activities.

QUESTION 74

Answer: A

Explanation: Utilizing a written survey allows for systematic feedback from all participants, ensuring a comprehensive evaluation of the collaborative activity's effectiveness.

QUESTION 75

Answer: A

Explanation: Providing a written report with detailed information allows for clear and comprehensive communication between the special education teacher and the speech therapist regarding the student's characteristics and needs.

QUESTION 76

Answer: C

Explanation: Distributing a written survey to all participants allows for systematic feedback from a larger group, ensuring a comprehensive evaluation of the workshop's success.

QUESTION 77

Answer: B

Explanation: Collaborating with healthcare professionals through scheduled meetings allows for thorough discussions and planning to address Mia's medical needs effectively.

QUESTION 78

Answer: D

Explanation: Utilizing a written survey for all participants allows for systematic and anonymous feedback, ensuring a comprehensive evaluation of the collaborative event's success.

QUESTION 79

Answer: B

Explanation: Joining a professional organization specific to deaf education allows you to actively engage with professionals in the field and access valuable resources and knowledge to benefit your students.

QUESTION 80

Answer: C

Explanation: Subscribing to specialized journals and participating in webinars in the field of deaf education allows you to access current research and best practices, promoting your professional growth and development.

QUESTION 81

Answer: C

Explanation: Actively participating in a national association for deaf education demonstrates your commitment to upholding high standards by engaging with professionals and resources dedicated to the field.

QUESTION 82

Answer: C

Explanation: Membership in a professional association specific to deaf education is a valuable resource for accessing the latest evidence-based practices and strategies in the field, promoting your professional growth and development.

80

QUESTION 83

Answer: C

Explanation: Actively participating in a national association for deaf educators demonstrates your commitment to upholding high standards by engaging with professionals and resources specific to the field of deaf education.

QUESTION 84

Answer: D

Explanation: Subscribing to a specialized journal in deaf education and participating in online courses provide ongoing support and opportunities for professional development, helping you stay informed and grow in your practice.

QUESTION 85

Answer: C

Explanation: In this scenario, recognizing the cultural and linguistic differences and leveraging the student's familiarity with ASL can be an effective strategy. Collaborating with the family to incorporate ASL into English reading lessons can help bridge the gap and improve the student's reading comprehension.

QUESTION 86

Answer: A

Explanation: Providing written instructions ensures that the student has access to information in a way that accommodates their hearing impairment, without solely relying on hearing aids or interpreters. This approach supports the student's understanding of assignments.

QUESTION 87

Answer: B

Explanation: Providing peer buddies who know sign language can help bridge the communication gap and promote social inclusion for the deaf student. It allows the student to engage in meaningful interactions with peers who understand their communication needs.

QUESTION 88

Answer: C

Explanation: To support the development of English language skills, it's essential to provide targeted tutoring and practice in English. While ASL is valuable, focusing on English language skills is necessary for academic success in an English-speaking environment.

QUESTION 89

Answer: C

Explanation: In this scenario, allowing students to choose their preferred communication method (ASL or visual communication system) promotes inclusivity and respects their individual needs and preferences. This approach ensures equal participation and fosters a sense of belonging.

QUESTION 90

Answer: C

Explanation: Collaborating with the student's family to incorporate their sign language into English reading lessons recognizes the importance of the student's cultural and linguistic background. This strategy can bridge the gap between languages and improve the student's reading comprehension in English.

QUESTION 91

Answer: A

Explanation: Providing the student with a noise-canceling headset can significantly reduce background noise, making it easier for the student to focus on classroom discussions and overcome the challenges related to their hearing impairment. This accommodation promotes inclusion within the regular classroom environment.

QUESTION 92

Answer: D

Explanation: Limited access to auditory input due to profound hearing loss can significantly impact a child's ability to acquire clear speech. Even with consistent therapy, the lack of auditory feedback may result in speech difficulties.

QUESTION 93

Answer: B

Explanation: The student's proficiency in reading and writing suggests strong language and cognitive abilities. However, their struggles with expressive spoken language may stem from a lack of support for sign language communication in the mainstream classroom, which hinders their language development.

QUESTION 94

Answer: C

Explanation: Both students, despite the difference in the degree of hearing loss, may experience delayed speech and language milestones compared to their typically developing peers. Hearing loss can affect speech and language development in various ways.

QUESTION 95

Answer: D

Explanation: Visual supports and clear enunciation can be effective strategies to support the speech development of a student with cochlear implants in a noisy and communicatively demanding context like a school play.

QUESTION 96

Answer: B

Explanation: Insufficiently advanced hearing technologies, such as outdated or malfunctioning cochlear implants or hearing aids, can hinder a student's ability to discriminate speech sounds, even when they are motivated and exposed to spoken language.

QUESTION 97

Answer: B

Explanation: Recognizing and accommodating the individual learning styles of each student allows for tailored instruction that can enhance cognitive development. A one-size-fits-all approach may not effectively address the diverse needs of these students.

QUESTION 98

Answer: C

Explanation: Combining visual aids with text-based materials can provide additional support for a visual learner's reading comprehension. This approach enhances understanding while still engaging the student with text.

QUESTION 99

Answer: B

Explanation: Leveraging a spatial learner's strengths involves providing hands-on, interactive activities and manipulatives. This approach helps enhance cognitive development by aligning with their preferred learning style.

QUESTION 100

Answer: B

Explanation: Engaging the student in group activities that align with their preferred learning style can foster socialization and peer relationships. This approach supports their social development by building on their strengths.

QUESTION 101

Answer: A

Explanation: Given Javier's proficiency in social studies and his need for additional support in mathematics, advocating for a mainstream classroom placement with appropriate supports for his hearing impairment and providing additional support in mathematics, while offering advanced coursework in social studies, would allow him to excel academically while addressing his areas of need.

QUESTION 102

Answer: A

Explanation: Facilitating structured peer interactions can help Emma and her classmates build effective communication skills and establish meaningful connections. This approach promotes Emma's integration into the mainstream classroom while also fostering a supportive and inclusive learning environment.

QUESTION 103

Answer: A

Explanation: Implementing a system of visual cues can provide clear communication of expectations for Jacob, helping him understand what is expected. Additionally, positive reinforcement for appropriate behavior helps motivate and reinforce socially acceptable conduct, creating a more conducive learning environment for Jacob and his classmates.

QUESTION 104

Answer: A

Explanation: Creating opportunities for one-on-one interactions and actively listening to Sarah's thoughts and concerns can help build trust and rapport. This approach acknowledges Sarah's individuality and supports her in developing meaningful connections with her teachers.

QUESTION 105

Answer: A

Explanation: Providing visual schedules and cues can offer Elena a structured visual framework to anticipate and navigate classroom routines effectively. This approach supports her in adapting to the classroom environment and promotes a positive learning experience.

QUESTION 106

Answer: A

Explanation: Encouraging Mark to use assistive technology tools aligns with his interest in technology and can help him overcome communication barriers. This approach empowers Mark to actively participate in classroom activities and reduces frustration.

QUESTION 107

Answer: A

Explanation:

Encouraging James to use humor in a positive and inclusive way can help him connect with his peers and establish rapport. This approach leverages James' natural disposition to support his social integration in the classroom.

QUESTION 108

Answer: A

Explanation: Specialized organizations that focus on producing educational materials for students with hearing impairments are likely to have resources and materials tailored to meet the specific needs of students like Maria. These materials can support her in conducting hands-on science experiments.

QUESTION 109

Answer: A

Explanation: Online resources provided by organizations dedicated to creating accessible educational materials are likely to offer historical content in formats that are accessible to students with hearing impairments. These resources can help Alex engage with historical content in a meaningful way.

QUESTION 110

Answer: A

Explanation: Art supply stores that specifically cater to the needs of students with sensory disabilities are likely to carry specialized art supplies suitable for students like Sophia. These supplies are designed to accommodate the unique needs of individuals who are deaf or hard of hearing.

QUESTION 111

Answer: A

Explanation: Organizations or agencies specializing in assistive technology for individuals with hearing impairments are likely to have a range of specialized devices and resources tailored to meet the specific needs of students like James. These resources can further enhance his educational experience.

QUESTION 112

Answer: A

Explanation: Given Michael's proficiency in lip reading and spoken language, a multisensory approach that combines visual cues with spoken language can reinforce comprehension and address his educational needs effectively. This approach acknowledges and builds upon his existing communication skills.

QUESTION 113

Answer: A

Explanation: Emma's strong proficiency in expressive sign language suggests that incorporating visual supports and graphic organizers can effectively facilitate her comprehension of written language. This evidence-based practice builds upon her existing strengths while addressing her specific needs in written communication.

QUESTION 114

Answer: A

Explanation: Given Sophie's proficiency in both sign language and written English, providing visual and written supports for auditory content can enhance her comprehension. This instructional method leverages her existing communication skills while addressing her specific needs in processing auditory information.

QUESTION 115

Answer: A

Explanation: Liam's challenges in articulation and phonological skills indicate that implementing speech therapy sessions focused on these areas can be highly effective. This evidence-based practice targets Liam's specific communication needs and aims to improve his spoken language proficiency.

QUESTION 116

Answer: A

Explanation: Given Nina's proficiency in both sign language and written English, providing visual and written supports for complex auditory content can enhance her comprehension. This instructional method leverages her existing communication skills while addressing her specific needs in processing complex auditory information.

QUESTION 117

Answer: A

Explanation: Evan's challenges in understanding complex written material indicate a need for targeted reading instruction. Implementing a structured approach that addresses his specific difficulties in this area is an evidence-based practice to support his educational progress in reading comprehension.

QUESTION 118

Answer: A

Explanation: Facilitating structured peer interactions that incorporate ASL allows Emily to effectively communicate with her classmates. This approach promotes Emily's integration into the mainstream classroom while also fostering a supportive and inclusive learning environment.

QUESTION 119

Answer: A

Explanation: Encouraging Joshua to reflect on his learning preferences, strengths, and areas of need empowers him to actively participate in his IEP meetings. This self-awareness enhances his ability to advocate for his educational needs effectively.

QUESTION 120

Answer: A

Explanation: Providing Lila with opportunities for role-playing and practicing social interactions in a supportive environment allows her to develop and refine her social skills in preparation for her involvement in the drama club. This approach empowers Lila to engage in social activities with confidence.

QUESTION 121

Answer: A

Explanation: Encouraging Miguel to explore various career options, interests, and skills through internships and vocational assessments enhances his self-awareness and helps him make informed decisions about his future. This approach empowers Miguel to take an active role in planning for his post-secondary education and career.

QUESTION 122

Answer: A

Explanation: Providing opportunities for Olivia to take on leadership roles and make decisions in collaborative projects allows her to further develop her assertiveness and sense of responsibility. This approach recognizes and nurtures Olivia's existing strengths and qualities.

QUESTION 123

Answer: A

Explanation: Encouraging Isaac to actively participate in cooking and budgeting activities while providing guidance and support as needed allows him to further enhance his independence and practical life skills. This approach empowers Isaac to develop essential skills for daily living.

QUESTION 124

Answer: A

Explanation: Actively involving Jamie's family in the development of their IEP is crucial to ensure that their cultural and linguistic preferences are considered. This approach demonstrates respect for Jamie's cultural background and reinforces the importance of collaboration between home and school.

QUESTION 125

Answer: A

Explanation: Implementing strategies to provide information and communicate with Mila's parents in their native language is crucial for ensuring they are informed and involved in her education. This approach helps bridge the language gap and facilitates meaningful collaboration between home and school.

QUESTION 126

Answer: A

Explanation: Establishing open and regular communication with both of Ethan's parents is crucial for gathering insights and addressing any concerns related to his well-being and academic progress. This approach ensures that the teacher is informed about Ethan's situation and can provide the necessary support during this transitional period.

QUESTION 127

Answer: A

Explanation: Encouraging Aiden's parents to actively participate in school activities and collaborate with the teacher aligns with their value for education. This approach reinforces learning at home and strengthens the partnership between home and school.

QUESTION 128

Answer: A

Explanation: Engaging in open and respectful dialogue with Sophie's parents is crucial for gaining a deeper understanding of their cultural values. Finding ways to integrate these values into the educational experience demonstrates respect for the family's perspective and promotes a collaborative approach between home and school.

QUESTION 129

Answer: A

Explanation: In this decision-making process, it is crucial to consider how each approach aligns with the unique needs and goals of individual students who are deaf or hard of hearing. A person-centered planning approach emphasizes tailoring education to individual students, which is essential for their success.

QUESTION 130

Answer: A

Explanation: Aiden's parents play a critical role in advocating for his educational needs. This includes seeking clarification on their rights under IDEA and actively participating in the IEP process to ensure Aiden receives the appropriate support and services.

QUESTION 131

Answer: A

Explanation: Sophia's parents should be aware of the right to a Free Appropriate Public Education (FAPE), which ensures that Sophia receives an education tailored to her needs at no cost to her parents. This legal standard protects the educational rights of students with disabilities, including those who are hard of hearing.

QUESTION 132

Answer: A

Explanation: The Smith family should be aware of their right to participate in and consent to the evaluation process for special education services. This includes providing input on assessment tools and methods used to determine Liam's eligibility and educational needs.

QUESTION 133

Answer: A

Explanation: Ella's parents should take the critical step of communicating their concerns to the school and requesting an IEP team meeting to discuss potential alternative placements. This collaborative approach allows for open dialogue and consideration of the best educational placement for Ella.

QUESTION 134

Answer: A

Explanation: Mateo's parents should be aware of their right to be actively involved in the referral and assessment process for special education services. This includes providing input and consent for evaluations, ensuring that Mateo's needs are properly assessed and addressed.

QUESTION 135

Answer: A

Explanation: Maintaining Sarah's records in a secure location accessible only to authorized personnel and ensuring that any electronic records are password-protected is crucial for preserving confidentiality. This approach aligns with legal and ethical guidelines.

QUESTION 136

Answer: A

Explanation: Providing Alex's parents with access to his records while redacting sensitive information about other students is an appropriate step to balance Alex's privacy with his parents' right to be informed about his progress.

QUESTION 137

Answer: A

Explanation: Respecting Emma's family's cultural values while maintaining accurate records involves seeking consent from her parents before sharing any information related to her progress or educational plan. This approach honors their privacy preferences.

QUESTION 138

Answer: A

Explanation: A critical consideration for Daniel in advocating for his own access to his educational records is familiarizing himself with his rights under FERPA and understanding how to request and review his records. This empowers him to take an active role in managing his educational information.

QUESTION 139

Answer: D

Explanation: Combining visual aids and multimedia with written materials can support the development of reading skills for an auditory learner. This approach integrates their preferred learning style with reading practice.

QUESTION 140

Answer: B

Explanation: Recognizing and accommodating diverse learning styles allows teachers to tailor instruction to individual needs, optimizing each student's learning potential. It promotes inclusive teaching and fosters better learning outcomes.

QUESTION 141

Answer: C

Explanation: In this case, the most effective approach is to create a lesson that incorporates elements of all three learning styles (tactile, visual, and auditory). This approach caters to the individual preferences of the students, ensuring an inclusive learning experience.

QUESTION 142

Answer: B

Explanation: Encouraging the student to observe and document experiments visually aligns with their preferred learning style. This approach ensures active participation in the project while catering to their strengths.

QUESTION 143

Answer: C

Explanation: Providing hands-on activities and projects related to the curriculum allows the student to engage their spatial learning style while addressing academic topics. This approach can enhance their understanding of the material and improve their academic performance.

QUESTION 144

Answer: B

Explanation: Allowing the student to respond to assessment s in ASL recognizes their communication mode and provides an accessible means of assessment, aligning with their language proficiency.

QUESTION 145

Answer: B

Explanation: Using a variety of assessment formats that include visual and tactile elements ensures that the assessment is more accessible and accommodating of diverse backgrounds and learning styles among the students.

QUESTION 146

Answer: D

Explanation: Incorporating visual and written elements into the assessment ensures that it is accessible to students with varying degrees of hearing loss, providing multiple means of understanding and responding.

QUESTION 147

Answer: B

Explanation: To ensure cultural and linguistic sensitivity, it's essential to focus on assessments that align with the students' cultural backgrounds and experiences, which can improve fairness and validity.

QUESTION 148

Answer: A

Explanation: Administering the assessment in ASL aligns with the student's primary mode of communication and ensures accessibility for a deaf student who primarily uses ASL.

QUESTION 149

Answer: D

Explanation: Allowing students to choose their preferred mode of response (written English or sign language) provides a nonbiased approach that respects their communication preferences and abilities, ensuring a fair assessment of their writing skills.

QUESTION 150

Answer: B

Explanation: Assessing the student's reading comprehension through an ASL storytelling assessment aligns with their primary mode of communication and ensures a more accurate evaluation of their skills.

QUESTION 151

Answer: B

Explanation: Offering extended time allows the student with both hearing loss and a learning disability to demonstrate their writing skills without undue pressure, providing a fair assessment.

QUESTION 152

Answer: B

Explanation: A sign language storytelling assessment aligns with the students' primary mode of communication and is the most effective way to evaluate their reading fluency.

QUESTION 153

Answer: B

Explanation: Offering a choice between ASL and written English accommodates the diverse communication preferences of the students, ensuring a fair and unbiased assessment.

QUESTION 154

Answer: A

Explanation: Providing the assessment in written form accommodates the student's struggle with spoken language and aligns with their primary mode of communication, ensuring a fair assessment.

QUESTION 155

Answer: B

Explanation: Providing a speech-to-text software accommodates the student's strength in spoken language and can assist them in expressing their thoughts in writing, ensuring a more accurate assessment of their writing skills.

QUESTION 156

Answer: C

Explanation: Incorporating visual aids and gestures alongside spoken language ensures that both students, one with a cochlear implant and one using ASL, can access and understand the content, promoting inclusivity in the classroom.

QUESTION 157

Answer: D

Explanation: Positioning the student to optimize sound reception is a practical modification that helps the hard of hearing student make the most of their hearing aids and engage in classroom discussions effectively.

QUESTION 158

Answer: C

Explanation: Fostering self-advocacy skills and offering appropriate accommodations empowers the student to actively participate in the classroom and develop independence, which is vital for their long-term success.

QUESTION 159

Answer: C

Explanation: Implementing peer tutoring and involving classmates in supporting the student fosters a sense of belonging and promotes active participation by creating a supportive and inclusive classroom community.

QUESTION 160

Answer: D

Explanation: Using a microphone and speaker system ensures that the student with a cochlear implant can access and understand group discussions more effectively, facilitating their active participation.

QUESTION 161

Answer: C

Explanation: Providing information and encouraging the student to request support services fosters self-advocacy and independence, empowering them to actively participate in their own education.

QUESTION 162

Answer: D

Explanation: Implementing a microphone and speaker system helps overcome background noise, making group discussions more accessible to both students. It creates an inclusive learning environment without isolating them or relying solely on written communication.

QUESTION 163

Answer: D

Explanation: Using a microphone and speaker system ensures that the student can access and understand group discussions more effectively, facilitating their active participation despite their hearing aids.

90

QUESTION 164

Answer: C

Explanation: Incorporating a variety of teaching methods, visual aids, and written materials accommodates the diverse needs of the students, ensuring an inclusive learning environment that caters to various communication preferences and abilities.

QUESTION 165

Answer: C

Explanation: Offering ASL-based reading materials and comprehension support addresses the student's specific needs and utilizes their strengths in ASL for improved reading comprehension.

QUESTION 166

Answer: C

Explanation: To differentiate instruction effectively, it's crucial to identify each student's unique strengths and weaknesses and adjust teaching methods to meet their individual needs.

QUESTION 167

Answer: C

Explanation: Creating flexible learning groups based on language proficiency allows for differentiated instruction that caters to the individual needs and language abilities of the students.

QUESTION 168

Answer: C

Explanation: Incorporating assistive technology aligns with research-based methods and can provide effective support for a student with writing difficulties, including those with additional learning disabilities.

QUESTION 169

Answer: B

Explanation: Consulting with a team of specialists helps ensure that instructional materials are research-based and tailored to the unique needs of students who are deaf or hard of hearing.

QUESTION 170

Answer: B

Explanation: Incorporating both visual and auditory elements in reading instruction aligns with research-based methods and caters to the student's cochlear implant use, enhancing their reading skills through multiple modalities.

QUESTION 171

Answer: C

Explanation: ASL relies on facial expressions and non-manual markers for conveying meaning and grammar, so understanding their significance is crucial for effective communication and support.

QUESTION 172

Answer: C

Explanation: ASL has its own distinct syntax and sentence structure that differ from English. Prioritizing this aspect helps students understand and use ASL effectively.

QUESTION 173

Answer: C

Explanation: Providing instruction that explicitly compares and contrasts ASL and English helps the student understand the linguistic differences and improves their English language skills while respecting their primary mode of communication.

QUESTION 174

Answer: B

Explanation: Highlighting the SVO word order in ASL as opposed to the subject-verb-object word order in English is a fundamental distinction that helps students understand the differences in sentence structure.

QUESTION 175

Answer: C

Explanation: Emphasizing the rich use of classifiers in ASL to convey specific meanings showcases the depth and complexity of ASL linguistics and enhances students' understanding of the language.

QUESTION 176

Answer: C

Explanation: Creating flexible learning groups based on ASL proficiency levels allows for differentiated instruction that accommodates the varying levels of ASL proficiency among students, promoting inclusivity in the classroom.

QUESTION 177

Answer: C

Explanation: Tailoring vocational training to match students' individual interests and abilities maximizes their potential for vocational competence and success.

QUESTION 178

Answer: B

Explanation: Consulting with the student to identify relevant materials and resources empowers them to pursue their career interests effectively, promoting vocational competence.

QUESTION 179

Answer: C

Explanation: Offering real-life situations and decision-making opportunities allows students to practice and develop functional living skills, preparing them for independent living.

QUESTION 180

Answer: C

Explanation: Selecting assistive technologies that cater to the unique needs of deaf individuals ensures their effective communication and vocational skill development.

QUESTION 181

Answer: C

Explanation: Model programs provide special education teachers with valuable strategies and best practices that have been effective for deaf and hard of hearing students, benefiting their educational success.

QUESTION 182

Answer: C

Explanation: Selecting a program that aligns with the unique needs of the deaf and hard of hearing children ensures that they receive appropriate and effective early childhood education.

QUESTION 183

Answer: C

Explanation: Engaging in open communication with the parents allows for a collaborative decision-making process and provides the parents with information to make an informed choice that aligns with their preferences and the child's needs.

QUESTION 184

Answer: C

Explanation: Conducting a comprehensive assessment allows for a thorough understanding of the student's needs, strengths, and areas requiring intervention, addressing the parents' concerns more effectively.

QUESTION 185

Answer: C

Explanation: Implementing peer support and fostering an inclusive classroom community helps address the student's feelings of isolation, promoting their social and emotional well-being.

QUESTION 186

Answer: C

Explanation: Providing resources and training to the parents to learn ASL facilitates effective communication between the student and their parents, enhancing their family relationship.

QUESTION 187

Answer: C

Explanation: Collaborating with the student and parents to identify accommodations and support for extracurricular participation allows the student to engage fully in activities while addressing their concerns.

QUESTION 188

Answer: C

Explanation: Holding a meeting with the parents to discuss their concerns and involve them in the transition plan promotes a smooth transition for the student while addressing parental concerns.

QUESTION 189

Answer: C

Explanation: Collaborative planning and co-teaching with the general education teacher is an effective strategy to provide support and coach them in accommodating the deaf student's needs.

QUESTION 190

Answer: C

Explanation: Coaching general education teachers to promote differentiated instruction and individualized accommodations ensures that they cater to the unique needs of each deaf or hard of hearing student.

QUESTION 191

Answer: C

Explanation: Collaborating with the teacher and providing training on the assistive technologies is an effective coaching strategy, ensuring that the teacher can support the student effectively within the general education classroom.

QUESTION 192

Answer: C

Explanation: Coaching general education teachers to seamlessly integrate accommodations and technologies into the classroom promotes a more inclusive and effective learning environment.

QUESTION 193

Answer: C

Explanation: Promoting the use of visual aids and ASL interpreters is a key strategy to facilitate effective communication and inclusivity for a deaf student using ASL.

QUESTION 194

Answer: C

Explanation: Coaching special education teachers to build collaborative partnerships with community agencies and align services with students' individual needs ensures effective support and services for deaf and hard of hearing students.

QUESTION 195

Answer: C

Explanation: Regularly evaluating teaching practices and seeking feedback from various sources, including colleagues and students, is a key strategy for self-assessment and professional growth.

QUESTION 196

Answer: B

Explanation: To identify cultural biases, it's crucial to acknowledge and critically examine your own biases as a starting point for reflection and self-assessment.

QUESTION 197

Answer: B

Explanation: Reflecting on the situation, acknowledging the bias, and adjusting your teaching approach is the most effective immediate action to address unintentional bias and ensure fairness.

QUESTION 198

Answer: C

Explanation: Setting clear goals for professional growth and regularly evaluating progress through self-assessment are essential strategies for improving instruction.

QUESTION 199

Answer: B

Explanation: Interacting with deaf adults is crucial for gaining insights into deaf culture and language, which can significantly enhance communication skills with deaf and hard of hearing students.

QUESTION 200

Answer: B

Explanation: Seeking guidance and mentorship from experienced deaf adults or educators is a valuable strategy to enhance your communication skills and better support the newly enrolled deaf student.

QUESTION 201

Answer: D

Explanation: Deaf individuals often develop strong visual-spatial skills, which can enhance non-verbal cognitive abilities. This can lead to variations in language development without necessarily indicating a language processing disorder or cognitive impairment.

QUESTION 202

Answer: B

Explanation: IEPs are designed to address individual educational needs, and they will be tailored to each student's specific requirements, regardless of disability status.

QUESTION 203

Answer: B

Explanation: Learning ASL together can enhance family communication, build a sense of inclusion, and support the child's linguistic and social development.

QUESTION 204

Answer: C

Explanation: Adolescence is a time of significant social and emotional development, which can affect academic performance for all students, including those who are deaf or hard of hearing.

QUESTION 205

Answer: A

Explanation: Relying solely on lip-reading may restrict the child's access to a full and rich language, potentially impacting their overall development.

QUESTION 206

Answer: C

Explanation: Inclusive practices, along with efforts to build peer support and understanding, can significantly reduce social isolation experienced by deaf students in mainstream classrooms.

QUESTION 207

Answer: B

Explanation: It's essential to support Sarah's cultural and linguistic identity while also addressing her academic and social needs. A balanced approach that values her deaf identity and provides appropriate academic and social support is crucial for her development.

QUESTION 208

Answer: C

Explanation: Mark's academic profile suggests that his learning style and strengths may vary. Providing targeted support tailored to his needs, such as additional support in reading and writing, can help him succeed academically.

QUESTION 209

Answer: C

Explanation: To promote social inclusion, it's essential for the teacher to implement inclusive practices that facilitate communication and interaction between Alex and his hearing peers. This approach helps create a supportive and inclusive classroom environment.

QUESTION 210

Answer: C

Explanation: This observation likely indicates that the child's receptive ASL skills (comprehension) are developing at a different rate than their expressive skills (signing), which is a common aspect of sign language development.

QUESTION 211

Answer: C

Explanation: Since the child's parents have chosen not to use hearing aids or cochlear implants, exploring alternative communication options, such as sign language, can be crucial for the child's educational success.

QUESTION 212

Answer: B

Explanation: Sign Supported English (SSE) relies on English grammar and vocabulary, so insufficient exposure to English text can hinder English language literacy development for deaf students using SSE.

QUESTION 213

Answer: B

Explanation: The age at which hearing loss occurs can significantly impact language development and learning experiences. Early identification and intervention are crucial for language development in deaf and hard of hearing children.

QUESTION 214

Answer: C

Explanation: Proficiency in ASL storytelling may positively influence narrative skills, but it may also have an impact on the development of English reading comprehension skills, potentially leading to variations in performance.

QUESTION 215

Answer: B

Explanation: Respecting and integrating the student's cultural and linguistic background, including their ties to the deaf community, is essential for creating an inclusive and supportive educational environment.

QUESTION 216

Answer: B

Explanation: Early and meaningful exposure to ASL can significantly benefit a deaf child's linguistic and cognitive development, promoting age-appropriate skills.

QUESTION 217

Answer: B

Explanation: Early intervention services are crucial for language development in deaf and hard of hearing children. The absence of such services may result in language delays that impact reading comprehension.

QUESTION 218

Answer: B

Explanation: Proficiency in ASL does not necessarily guarantee proficiency in written English, as they are separate language systems with different rules and structures.

QUESTION 219

Answer: C

Explanation: Providing language-rich environments and alternative communication methods are essential for supporting the language development of students who have experienced a lack of early language exposure.

QUESTION 220

Answer: B

Explanation: Early intervention services combined with a language-rich environment can significantly benefit the linguistic and cognitive development of hard of hearing children, promoting age-appropriate skills.

QUESTION 221

Answer: B

Explanation: Introducing ASL can offer Emily an additional means of communication and may complement her language development. It can provide her with a richer linguistic environment and potentially bridge any gaps in her language skills.

QUESTION 222

Answer: B

Explanation: Introducing sign language as a supplementary mode of communication can enhance Alex's language skills without necessarily hindering his speech development. It can offer him an additional tool for effective communication.

QUESTION 223

Answer: A

Explanation: While ASL is valuable, the family should consider that strong ASL skills may impact Sarah's motivation or time available for developing English literacy skills. A balance between both languages is often beneficial for academic success.

QUESTION 224

Answer: C

Explanation: An audiogram is a formal assessment tool used to measure a student's auditory abilities, including auditory discrimination and sound identification.

QUESTION 225

Answer: C

Explanation: Standardized articulation tests are specifically designed to assess a student's articulation and speech production skills.

QUESTION 226

Answer: C

Explanation: Standardized receptive language tests are designed to assess a student's ability to understand and follow spoken instructions.

QUESTION 227

Answer: B

Explanation: When assessing students with additional disabilities, it's crucial to consider their cognitive level and choose assessments that are appropriate and accessible for them.

QUESTION 228

Answer: B

Explanation: Informal assessments can include observations of a student's ability to follow spoken directions, which provides insights into their auditory skills.

QUESTION 229

Answer: C

Explanation: When assessing students with physical disabilities, it's essential to modify assessment methods to accommodate their specific needs and limitations, ensuring a fair and accurate evaluation.

QUESTION 230

Answer: C

Explanation: A student who excels in reading comprehension despite decoding challenges may have developed strong compensatory strategies to compensate for their difficulties in decoding.

QUESTION 231

Answer: B

Explanation: Effective communication with parents involves providing a clear and simplified summary of assessment results with explanations that are easy to understand.

QUESTION 232

Answer: C

Explanation: The results suggest that while the student has creativity and storytelling abilities, they may need targeted support to improve their grammatical accuracy.

QUESTION 233

Answer: C

Explanation: Celebrating achievements and setting new goals can motivate the student and foster a positive attitude towards their progress.

QUESTION 234

Answer: B

Explanation: When a student struggles with both decoding and reading comprehension, it may indicate a significant reading disability that requires targeted interventions.

QUESTION 235

Answer: C

Explanation: Collaborating and discussing the results together with the general education teacher can lead to a better understanding of the student's needs and the development of appropriate strategies and support.

QUESTION 236

Answer: A

Explanation: When a student shows difficulties in both decoding and reading comprehension, it is indicative of a potential severe reading disability. Mr. Johnson should consider this interpretation and recommend appropriate interventions to support Sarah's reading development.

QUESTION 237

Answer: C

Explanation: Celebrating achievements and setting new goals during a meeting with John's parents is a positive and collaborative approach to sharing assessment results and maintaining a supportive educational environment.

QUESTION 238

Answer: C

Explanation: Collaborating with the general education teacher to discuss the results and develop targeted strategies can lead to a better understanding of Maria's needs and the development of appropriate support plans to address her reading comprehension challenges.

QUESTION 239

Answer: B

Explanation: Bright, glare-free lighting is crucial for creating a visual-friendly environment, allowing deaf students to access visual information effectively.

QUESTION 240

Answer: C

Explanation: A visual schedule with clear cues is a valuable strategy for helping deaf and hard of hearing students navigate transitions effectively, as it provides visual support and predictability.

QUESTION 241

Answer: C

Explanation: Induction loop systems are crucial for ensuring that hearing aid users can access auditory information effectively in the classroom, enhancing auditory learning opportunities.

QUESTION 242

Answer: C

Explanation: Clear expectations and routines for classroom behavior can help minimize disruptions, optimize instructional time, and provide structure, which is especially important for students who are deaf or hard of hearing.

QUESTION 243

Answer: B

Explanation: Providing written transcripts of spoken instructions benefits both deaf and hearing students by offering visual support and improving access to information.

QUESTION 244

Answer: C

Explanation: A visual schedule with clear time frames is a critical strategy to provide structure and predictability, helping deaf and hard of hearing students transition smoothly between lessons.

QUESTION 245

Answer: B

Explanation: Encouraging the student to apply the skill in real-world contexts helps promote generalization, allowing the student to transfer their knowledge and abilities beyond the classroom setting.

QUESTION 246

Answer: D

Explanation: Encouraging the student to set personal goals and create a schedule promotes self-assessment, self-advocacy, and metacognitive skills, enabling them to take control of their time management and organization.

QUESTION 247

Answer: C

Explanation: Collaborating with the family to reinforce communication skills at home is crucial for facilitating skill generalization across different learning environments.

QUESTION 248

Answer: B

Explanation: Teaching the student to break down complex instructions into smaller, manageable steps is a valuable metacognitive strategy that can improve comprehension and problem-solving.

QUESTION 249

Answer: C

Explanation: Creating opportunities for the student to practice skills in different contexts helps foster generalization and ensures that the student can apply their abilities across various learning environments.

QUESTION 250

Answer: B

Explanation: Teaching the student to identify and seek quiet spaces during noisy times is a valuable self-advocacy strategy to address their needs effectively in noisy classroom settings.

QUESTION 251

Answer: C

Explanation: Incorporating ASL signs alongside English vocabulary helps bridge the gap between the student's first language (ASL) and second language (English) by providing visual support and enhancing comprehension.

QUESTION 252

Answer: C

Explanation: Teaching comprehension strategies is essential for developing reading comprehension skills in deaf or hard of hearing students, as it helps them actively engage with the text and improve understanding.

QUESTION 253

Answer: C

Explanation: Teaching explicit strategies for transferring writing skills from ASL to English helps the student bridge the gap between the two languages and effectively apply their skills in English writing.

100

QUESTION 254

Answer: C

Explanation: Providing explicit instruction on English grammar rules and structures is essential for helping deaf students learn the grammar of their second language effectively.

QUESTION 255

Answer: C

Explanation: Implementing repeated oral reading of texts with appropriate feedback is an evidence-based strategy for improving reading fluency in students, including those who are deaf or hard of hearing.

QUESTION 256

Answer: C

Explanation: Providing explicit instruction on transferring writing skills from ASL to written English is a valuable approach for helping the student effectively apply their skills in written English.

QUESTION 257

Answer: B

Explanation: Encouraging the student to reach out independently by providing contact information empowers them to take charge of their own needs and resources.

QUESTION 258

Answer: C

Explanation: Regular meetings to discuss communication preferences and needs ensure that the student, interpreter, and teacher are aligned in their approach, leading to more effective communication.

QUESTION 259

Answer: C

Explanation: Facilitating a meeting to explain the transition and providing guidance on working with the new interpreter helps the student adapt smoothly and ensures effective communication.

QUESTION 260

Answer: C

Explanation: Offering hands-on guidance and practice in using relay services is the most effective way to ensure that the student can use them effectively when needed.

QUESTION 261

Answer: C

Explanation: Facilitating a meeting to address communication challenges and preferences involving the student, interpreter, and teacher is essential for finding effective solutions and improving the student's use of the interpreter.

QUESTION 262

Answer: C

Explanation: Offering training and practice sessions with the new speech-to-text interpreter helps the student adapt effectively to the transition and ensures successful communication in the new format.

QUESTION 263

Answer: C

Explanation: Encouraging parents to actively share their insights, concerns, and goals for their child is essential for their meaningful participation in the IEP process, leading to a more effective plan.

QUESTION 264

Answer: C

Explanation: Acknowledging and respecting cultural differences and adapting communication strategies as needed is essential for ensuring effective communication and collaboration among culturally diverse families, professionals, and community agencies.

QUESTION 265

Answer: C

Explanation: Arranging for qualified interpreters or bilingual professionals to facilitate communication ensures that language barriers do not hinder the parents' active participation in the IEP process.

QUESTION 266

Answer: C

Explanation: Engaging in open dialogue, respecting diverse perspectives, and seeking common ground are essential steps in fostering cultural responsiveness and effective collaboration among families with different cultural beliefs.

QUESTION 267

Answer: C

Explanation: Creating a welcoming and supportive environment, addressing concerns, and involving parents in decision-making can help rebuild trust and encourage their active participation in the IEP process.

QUESTION 268

Answer: B

Explanation: Thomas Hopkins Gallaudet is known for his pioneering work in advocating for manual communication methods and establishing the first American school for the deaf, contributing significantly to the historical foundations of deaf education.

QUESTION 269

Answer: D

Explanation: In educational contexts, "moderate hearing loss" is a term commonly used to describe a degree of hearing loss that ranges from mild to profound and often involves the use of hearing aids or assistive listening devices.

QUESTION 270

Answer: B

Explanation: Laurent Clerc, a deaf educator, played a pivotal role in establishing the first permanent public school for the deaf in the United States (Hartford School for the Deaf) and promoted the use of sign language as the primary mode of communication for deaf students.

QUESTION 271

Answer: C

Explanation: In educational terminology, "Hard of Hearing" is used to describe a person with a hearing loss who primarily communicates through spoken language, often with the support of hearing aids or cochlear implants.

QUESTION 272

Answer: D

Explanation: The Bicultural-Bilingual Approach in deaf education emphasizes the importance of fostering a strong Deaf cultural identity and using sign language as a primary mode of communication, alongside proficiency in written and spoken language.

QUESTION 273

Answer: A

Explanation: In educational contexts, "congenital hearing loss" is used to describe a hearing loss that is present at birth or acquired early in life, typically before the development of spoken language skills.

QUESTION 274

Answer: B

Explanation: The CEC Code of Ethics emphasizes the importance of advocating for the student's rights and well-being while maintaining confidentiality, ensuring that the student's needs are met.

QUESTION 275

Answer: C

Explanation: Designing the classroom to ensure equal access and accommodations for all students, including those who are deaf or hard of hearing, is essential for compliance with applicable laws and policies.

QUESTION 276

Answer: B

Explanation: The CEC Code of Ethics encourages professionals to advocate for the best interests of the student while respecting differing perspectives and working collaboratively with colleagues.

QUESTION 277

Answer: C

Explanation: When implementing accommodations for students who are deaf or hard of hearing, it is essential to ensure that the accommodations meet the specific needs of each student while adhering to testing policies to maintain fairness.

QUESTION 278

Answer: C

Explanation: The CEC Code of Ethics encourages professionals to address concerns directly with colleagues while maintaining confidentiality, as this approach promotes open communication and resolution.

QUESTION 279

Answer: C

Explanation: The primary objective when implementing communication accommodations should be to ensure that they effectively support the student's learning and participation, in compliance with legal requirements and individualized needs

QUESTION 280

Answer: A

Explanation: The cochlea is a spiral-shaped, fluid-filled structure in the inner ear. It contains hair cells that convert mechanical vibrations (sound waves) into electrical signals, which are then transmitted to the brain through the auditory nerve.

QUESTION 281

Answer: B

Explanation: The middle ear is responsible for amplifying sound vibrations and transmitting them to the inner ear. In a noisy environment, background noise can interfere with the transmission of sound through the middle ear, making it more challenging for the student to hear clearly.

QUESTION 282

Answer: A

Explanation: The outer ear, including the pinna, helps in sound localization by collecting sound waves from different directions. If there is an issue with the outer ear, the child may struggle to accurately determine the source of a sound.

QUESTION 283

Answer: A

Explanation: The cochlea is responsible for differentiating between different frequencies of sound. If a student has difficulty hearing high-frequency sounds, it suggests an issue with the cochlea.

QUESTION 284

Answer: B

Explanation: A cochlear implant is a device that directly stimulates the auditory nerve, bypassing the damaged or non-functioning hair cells in the inner ear (cochlea). This allows the individual to perceive sound.

QUESTION 285

Answer: C

Explanation: The startle response to loud noises is one of the earliest auditory skills to develop in infants. This indicates that their auditory system is functioning and they are sensitive to sound stimuli.

QUESTION 286

Answer: B

Explanation: This approach combines written instructions with sign language, providing multiple modalities of access for the student. It caters to their deafness while addressing their learning disability.

QUESTION 287

Answer: A

Explanation: Assigning individual tasks allows the student to focus without being overwhelmed by distractions in a group setting. This modification caters to both their deafness and ADHD.

QUESTION 288

Answer: A

Explanation: Students with ASD and hearing impairments may experience sensory overload, particularly in noisy environments. This can hinder their ability to focus and learn effectively.

QUESTION 289

Answer: A

Explanation: AAC devices can provide vital support for students with expressive language difficulties, allowing them to communicate effectively despite their challenges.

104

QUESTION 290

Answer: A

Explanation: To support a student with both hearing and mobility challenges, it's crucial to ensure their learning environment is physically accessible, with appropriate seating and workstations.

QUESTION 291

Answer: A

Explanation: Text-to-speech software can be a powerful tool for students with dyslexia and hearing impairments, as it provides auditory support for reading comprehension.

QUESTION 292

Answer: A

Explanation: Auditory discrimination involves the ability to perceive and differentiate various speech sounds. It is a crucial aspect of assessing a student's auditory processing abilities.

QUESTION 293

Answer: A

Explanation: Formal assessments may not capture a student's full range of communication skills, especially in natural, conversational settings. This limitation is particularly relevant for students who are hard of hearing.

QUESTION 294

Answer: A

Explanation: Articulation refers to the ability to produce speech sounds clearly and accurately. It is an important aspect to consider when assessing speech development in students who are deaf.

QUESTION 295

Answer: A

Explanation: A functional behavior assessment looks at the underlying causes of behaviors and can be particularly useful for students with complex needs, including those who are deaf and have additional disabilities.

QUESTION 296

Answer: C

Explanation: Considering the student's preferred mode of communication ensures that the assessment is conducted in a way that is accessible and meaningful to them, leading to a more accurate evaluation of their abilities.

QUESTION 297

Answer: A

Explanation: Language sample analysis involves collecting and analyzing samples of a student's spontaneous speech. This informal assessment can provide rich information about their language development, including vocabulary use, syntax, and discourse skills.

QUESTION 298

Answer: B

Explanation: Given that Jane primarily communicates through sign language, the written format of the test may not have been accessible to her. It's essential to consider alternative ways to assess her reading comprehension skills, such as through sign-supported English or a signed version of the test, to obtain a more accurate reflection of her abilities.

QUESTION 299

Answer: A

Explanation: A formal articulation assessment may not fully capture Mark's articulation abilities, as it may not consider the influence of his hearing impairment on his speech production. Informal assessments or observations in natural communication settings may provide a more comprehensive picture of his articulation skills.

QUESTION 300

Answer: B

Explanation: Sarah's preferred mode of communication and the accommodations provided during the assessment are essential factors to consider. The results may be influenced by whether she had access to sign language or other communication supports during the test. This information can help determine if the results accurately reflect her mathematical abilities or if they are affected by the assessment format and communication access.

QUESTION 301

Answer: C

Explanation: The audiogram results indicate the severity of Sarah's hearing loss in each ear. To effectively communicate with stakeholders, it's crucial to address the potential impact on her speech and language development and recommend appropriate interventions, such as speech therapy or sign language instruction, to support her learning.

QUESTION 302

Answer: C

Explanation: To support Alex's classroom participation, it's essential to communicate the assessment results to his teachers and recommend strategies such as preferential seating or FM systems, which can help him hear more clearly in noisy environments.

QUESTION 303

Answer: B

Explanation: Communicating that Emma's articulation skills are age-appropriate is important, but suggesting regular speech therapy as a strategy for continued speech development is beneficial. This approach encourages ongoing support and growth.

QUESTION 304

Answer: B

Explanation: To support James in a mainstream classroom, it's essential to communicate the assessment results and recommend strategies such as using visual aids and captioned materials to enhance his learning experience.

QUESTION 305

Answer: B

Explanation: Sharing positive assessment results with parents and teachers is important. Suggesting periodic monitoring to ensure continued progress encourages a collaborative approach and ongoing support for Sophia's speech development.

QUESTION 306

Answer: D

Explanation: Communicating the assessment results to Nathan's parents and teachers and recommending strategies such as auditory processing therapy and preferential seating can provide targeted support for his auditory processing difficulties in the classroom.

QUESTION 307

Answer: A

Explanation: Given Maria's proficiency in both sign language and spoken English, a bilingual education program that supports both modalities can provide a balanced approach to her education, addressing her strengths in mathematics while also providing support for written English.

QUESTION 308

Answer: A

Explanation: Given Ethan's strengths in hands-on activities and visual learning, a specialized program that incorporates these elements can provide him with the support and resources he needs to succeed academically, especially in areas where he may require additional assistance like reading comprehension.

QUESTION 309

Answer: A

Explanation: Given Raj's proficiency in ASL and strong academic skills, placing him in a mainstream classroom with appropriate supports for his deafness and providing advanced coursework in his areas of strength can help him reach his full potential academically and socially.

QUESTION 310

Answer: A

Explanation: Considering Aisha's strengths in expressive sign language, a program that builds on this proficiency while also providing support for written English can create a balanced approach to her education, addressing both her strengths and areas of need.

QUESTION 311

Answer: A

Explanation: Given Omar's passion and proficiency in visual arts, placing him in a general education classroom and providing additional support for language arts can allow him to thrive academically while also nurturing his artistic talents.

QUESTION 312

Answer: A

Explanation: Given Leila's high motivation and above-average performance in all subjects, placing her in a mainstream classroom with appropriate supports for her deafness and providing opportunities for advanced coursework can help her excel academically and reach her full potential.

QUESTION 313

Answer: A

Explanation: Given Alex's proficiency in ASL and his struggles with written English, a bilingual education program that supports both modalities, along with continued support in mathematics, would provide a balanced approach to his education, addressing both his strengths and areas of need.

QUESTION 314

Answer: A

Explanation: Given Sophie's proficiency in science and her need for additional support in English language arts, enrolling her in a mainstream classroom with appropriate supports for her hearing loss and providing additional support in English language arts, while offering advanced coursework in science, would allow her to excel academically while addressing her areas of need.

QUESTION 315

Answer: A

Explanation: A critical step for Jaden's teacher is to establish clear protocols for storing and accessing his records, ensuring that only authorized personnel have access. This respects Jaden's community values while maintaining confidentiality.

QUESTION 316

Answer: A

Explanation: In response to Olivia's desire for increased involvement, her teacher should collaborate with her to provide guidance on how to request and review her records. This empowers Olivia to take an active role in managing her educational information.

www.ingramcontent.com/pod-product-compliance
Lightning Source LLC
LaVergne TN
LVHW082044210325
806549LV00004B/623